Wilfrid Philip Ward

The Wish to Believe

A Discussion concerning the Temper of Mind in which a reasonable Man should

undertake religious Inquiry

Wilfrid Philip Ward

The Wish to Believe
*A Discussion concerning the Temper of Mind in which a reasonable Man should undertake
religious Inquiry*

ISBN/EAN: 9783337130275

Printed in Europe, USA, Canada, Australia, Japan

Cover: Foto ©ninafisch / pixelio.de

More available books at **www.hansebooks.com**

THE

WISH TO BELIEVE

A DISCUSSION

CONCERNING THE TEMPER OF MIND IN WHICH A
REASONABLE MAN SHOULD UNDERTAKE
RELIGIOUS INQUIRY

BY

WILFRID WARD

" Thy wish was father, Harry, to that thought "
Shakespeare

" They dared not lightly believe what they so much wished to be true "
Arnold's " History of Rome "

LONDON

KEGAN PAUL, TRENCH, & CO., 1 PATERNOSTER SQUARE

1885

The first dialogue and a portion of the second appeared originally in the " Nineteenth Century," and are here reprinted by kind permission of the Editor.

RIGHT REVEREND DR. HERBERT VAUGHAN,

LORD BISHOP OF SALFORD.

My dear Lord,

    I take it as a great kindness that you have allowed me to inscribe your name in the beginning of this book. It gives a high sanction to my work, and will, I trust, bring a blessing on the cause it was designed to serve.

    It is also a satisfaction to me of a more personal nature to be thus enabled to make some acknowledgment of the kindness and friendship you have constantly shown me from the earliest years of my life until now.

    It is not likely I can ever forget all that I owe you; but I welcome an opportunity which makes it natural for me to express what you must know I feel. And if it seems at first sight unfitting, in acknowledgment of so much, to offer you what is so slight, it is, on the other hand, the very

*greatness of your kindness to me which has led
me to hope that the book will have for you some
value apart from its intrinsic merits.*

*A portion of it—the dialogue which stands
second in the volume—has a special connection
with yourself, as it was written whilst I was
staying with you at St. Bede's College in the
summer of 1882. And this calls to my mind
another thought—the last I shall mention—with
which I should wish to associate this dedication.
I mean that the events of that summer bring
back the remembrance of my father's friendship
for you, and remind me that if I wish to connect
my work in any way with his memory, I can
offer it to none so suitably as to yourself.*

Believe me,

My dear Lord,

Ever your affectionate Servant,

WILFRID WARD.

*Sherborne House, Basingstoke,
October 1884.*

CONTENTS.

—◆—

INTRODUCTION.

I WISH, by way of preface to the following Dialogues, to state as shortly and clearly as I am able the exact nature of the subject with which they deal, and its practical bearing.

It is generally recognised when a man first turns from one form of religious belief to another, or from a state of unbelief to belief of some sort, that an important element in the change of his mind is a sense of the beauty or of the consolations afforded by the new creed, or of the need in him which it answers, and his consequent wish to believe in it if possible. If we go back half a century to the Tractarian movement, we see in the history of all the leading minds which came over to the Catholic Church, that their love of the Church, their interest in its history, their sense of the union Rome so plausibly claimed with the Church of the past, or their admiration for the completeness of the Roman system,—all sources of a strong wish to believe in Rome if possible,—preceded by a considerable period their actual belief. Twelve years before Newman became a Catholic he wrote the following lines, well known to his admirers :—

> "Oh that thy creed were sound,
> For thou dost soothe the heart, thou Church of Rome,
> By thy unwearied watch and varied round
> Of service in thy Saviour's holy home."

And the same feeling, or substantially the same, is apparent throughout the pages of the old " British Critic," which represented the opinions of the most active-minded of those who took part in the movement. And to go to what is unhappily a commoner case in our own day, the case of one who is destitute of firm belief altogether, who has been so much puzzled by the plausible objections of Mr. Huxley or Mr. Spencer against the possibility of knowing anything at all about God or a future life, that his mind is blank of any conviction whatever in the matter ; it is commonly the case that, where religious belief is gained by such a one, his first step towards it is a sense of the need of it, of the assistance it would be to him if he could attain to it, of the importance of knowing that there is a God and a future life, and of guiding his life by that knowledge if perchance it *is* true, or other similar considerations. If there is no wish to believe, considering the difficulties with which every form of belief is beset, it seems plain that there will be no motive force sufficient to arouse the mind to active inquiry from the negative state which neither affirms nor denies, but remains passive, confessing that the whole thing is a riddle and a puzzle.

But when believers admit that the natural and in most cases the necessary condition of coming to believe is a strong previous "wish to believe," their opponents come forward at once with a charge which seems very plausible. Your religion, they say, implies belief in a certain set of facts proved by evidence ; this evidence is before all who take the trouble to look into it ; the one necessary condition in order that it may be judged of rightly is that it should be viewed with absolute impartiality ; that he who judges

B

of its value should have a mind free from all
prepossession in favour either of its sufficiency
or of its insufficiency. But to suppose that it
is necessary in order to believe that one should
approach the matter with a strong wish to believe, is to acknowledge that belief is irrational.
If an impartial judge finds the evidence insufficient, and one who has a wish to believe finds
it suffice for him, it is plain that his belief is not
reasonable, but is biassed by his wish ; that his
wish has been father to his thought.

This was George Eliot's view. All religious
belief seemed to her only the reflection of the
need in the human heart. The kingdom of
heaven, she says in " Romola," is not without us
as a fact, but within us as a great longing. Mill
speaks to the same effect in his posthumous
essays : " We are living in an age of weak
beliefs," he writes, "and in which such belief
as men have is much more determined by their
wish to believe than by any mental appreciation
of evidence :" and Tennyson, in his dramatic
monologue " Despair," puts the same thought
into the mouth of the infidel, who sees that

the God who seemed to our forefathers to fill
the earth with His glory, appears now to many
to be but the creation of the human need for an
object of supreme reverence.

" He is now but a cloud and a smoke who was once a pillar of fire,
The guess of a worm in the dust and the shadow of its desire."

This charge is so plausible and so paralysing
to the belief of one who cannot feel sure that it
is untrue, that it seems necessary to look carefully at it. And it is with the object of obtain-
ing a clearer view than is evident at first sight
of its exact worth and import that the following
dialogues were written. It is plain that the
inquirer who thinks his judgment unreliable
directly he detects in himself a strong wish to
believe in the religion he is investigating is at
once thrown back. He cannot proceed without
the wish, which is his great motive ; and yet he
is told that if he has the wish, his judgment of
the evidence is unreliable, and he has no right to
believe. And a similar thought may trouble the
mind of one who already possesses belief, when
for the first time he looks into its grounds
with care, to satisfy himself that they are solid.

He feels the wish to believe, very likely, strong within him, and fears from what is so confidently alleged, that this may be fatal against his having the power of judging soundly. When he further considers that—apart from those whose belief is thoughtless and unquestioning—the great mass of those who believe have the wish to believe, and the great mass of those who are indifferent and impartial have no firm belief in such matters, the conclusion threatens with painful vividness that religious belief is prejudice—the offspring, not of right reason, but of a bias which puts more into the reasons alleged than a fair-minded man would find in them.

In order to estimate more exactly the value of the charge which is here made, it is necessary to look more closely into its nature.

The religious inquirer is accused of want of candour ; of being biassed by his wishes. Does he necessarily plead guilty to either of these charges by allowing that he has had and has still a strong wish to believe ? I think not. The Romans had the intensest possible wish to believe the good news of the victory over

Hasdrubal at the Metaurus, but it did not bias their view of the evidence. On the contrary, it sharpened all their critical faculties. They sifted each report. They allowed no report to escape them. " They dared not lightly believe," says Arnold, " what they so much wished to be true." Here then I come to the main subject of my inquiry. The question resolves itself to this. Granting that earnest religious inquirers must have a strong wish to believe, is not the strong wish of an earnest man to believe in something of vast importance to himself and on which he will have constantly to act, the wish for a belief the whole value of which is felt to consist in its truth, rather a source of carefulness and accuracy, of caution in believing and of great industry in allowing no consideration to escape which may throw light on the matter, than of rashness or precipitation in believing ? And then I go a step farther and suggest that in a matter of vast importance where one answer to the question under consideration is looked upon as supremely good news and the other answer as supremely bad, a keen wish to believe in the former if possible, is inseparable from the vivid realisation of the importance of the matter and of its personal relation to the inquirer's happiness which is essential for that keenness of mind and that single eye for truth which are the necessary conditions of fair and far-sighted judgment.

Several instances illustrative of this fact appear in my Dialogues. I may give one here which came under my own close personal observation, and which is concerned with religious belief, though not with the conflict between belief and no belief. One with whom I was intimately acquainted and who was formerly an Anglican looked into the well-known Honorius case in years gone by, and before he had any thoughts of joining the Roman communion. He studied it conscientiously as a matter of history, with no bias at all, and came to the conclusion that the Catholic answer was sufficient. Later on, when it came upon him as a difficulty against what he much wished to believe—the divinity of the Roman Church—two things resulted : firstly, the Catholic answer, in the form in which he was acquainted with it, which had before seemed sufficient, now failed to satisfy him ; and secondly, his intense wish to find and to believe that the charge was not fatal against papal infallibility gave his mind such keenness as to make him find out for himself further answers on the Catholic side. Both his perceptive and his critical faculties were, alike, sharpened. Thus in the end he gained an assurance of a far deeper and more permanent kind than he had had before, once he had, under these new circumstances, satisfied himself with an answer. Here it is plain that the keen sense of the importance of the matter and of its effects on himself personally, which gave this new *stimulus* and power to his mind, was inseparably connected with his wish to believe that Honorius could be defended, and that Catholicism was true. The absence of the wish must imply the absence of this strong motive power to just judgment and keen insight. Thus, although it must be granted that there *is* a kind of wish to believe which, as being divorced from a sense of the importance to oneself of knowing the truth, may readily lead to the indulgence of a hobby and may be father to the thought, there seems to be another, and quite a different kind of wish, which is the necessary concomitant of a keen wish to know the truth in matters where one result is extremely beneficial to oneself. And although in strict accuracy of speech this wish cannot be said in itself to aid the mind, it is nevertheless an excellent sign of that disposition of mind which is most favourable for clear-sighted and far-sighted judgment.

The wish to believe being, then, in such cases the necessary concomitant of the keen wish to know the truth, it seems plain that the attitude of captious scepticism which is so prevalent in these days is not really a hopeful attitude for learning the truth at all. In fact, the tables may be turned on our accusers, and it may be said that just as there is a wish to believe which leads the mind to look only at the motives for belief, and consequently exaggerates their value, and becomes father to the thought, so there is a species of sceptical inquiry which is bent, often unconsciously, upon realizing vividly only the reasons for doubt, and which consequently leads to irrational disbelief as the other leads to irrational belief. And when the necessity of critical inquiry is urged, the answer seems to be, in this case as in the other, that it is not the captious scepticism which is bent on disproving, but the anxious scepticism of one who wishes to believe if only he can believe securely and truthfully, which is of real service ; and this is not, I think, if clearly understood, a paradox. The radical attitude of mind is a longing to know all truth in a matter of vast importance, and the wish that that knowledge shall prove for our happiness is inseparable from this, as is also the wish that it should be genuine knowledge and not an illusion. And in these wishes are contained the motives alike for active inquiry and rational scepticism.

It will be observed from what I have already said, that I make no attempt to show from the facts of the case that no Christians or theists *are* prejudiced, or believe with that light belief which is readily gained on insufficient motives and as readily lost again. My reason for this is that, apart even from the fact that it would carry me into a line of thought very different from that which I have pursued, I do not believe such an investigation of the phenomena of individual minds to be possible; and if it were possible, it seems doubtful how far it would tell in favour of the mass of those who profess Christianity. Religious belief is now more and more felt to be what it was so clearly recognised to be when the Gospel began to spread, a part of the individual's moral probation. When, as in the Middle Ages, faith was general, and was as much an acceptance of received facts as belief in America is now, the fact of which I speak was perhaps less generally felt. The Schoolmen formulated their irrefragable arguments, and he who doubted seemed more fool than knave. I remember coming in some scholastic volume across a passage in which the author excuses himself for not treating of the existence of God, and gives as his reason, " Quia de facillimis non est hic disputatio." In these days few who think would speak thus. It is the most certain of truths, but surely one most encompassed with difficulty.

This is what Cardinal Newman feels, and I
fancy many others with him. Belief, when the
Church was as visible as the sun in the heavens,
seemed so obvious a course that it was natural
to suppose that its motives were as plainly convincing as the very sight of one's eyes. Faith
would thus sometimes remain based really only
on an unquestioned tradition. But now, in
these days of scepticism and questioning, it is
surely not too much to say that the only faith
which will ultimately stand must be based upon
those sufficient grounds which cannot exist
without individual earnestness and certain moral
qualities and habits in the individual. Thus to
speak of any large body of men, classified by
reference to external profession as though they
were in a matter so personal and individual on
a similar footing, would be unreal and mislead-
ing. I am not at all concerned to show that
there may not be Catholics whose faith has—
through their own fault, no doubt—become
shallow, and whose attitude of mind is no
guarantee that they are judging truly. What I
am concerned in maintaining is that the attitude

of mind which the Church insists on—though it rests with the individual how far he attends to her voice—is an eminently reasonable attitude, and an excellent safeguard, even naturally speaking, against errors of judgment arising either from carelessness or from precipitation. And it must be borne in mind that although for the sake of clearness in discussion I have illustrated my thesis principally from the mind's perception and estimate of individual arguments for and against religious belief, the principle I endeavour to establish extends far beyond the instances I adduce, and far beyond mere explicit arguments capable of expression in words. It is acknowledged by most both of believers and of unbelievers that the mind is swayed in its ultimate decision on such matters by considerations far more numerous and subtle than any words can represent. The phenomena of the world and of the human heart in all their number and complexity are before believer and unbeliever alike. One man, taking them in and weighing them in his own way, pronounces the reasons for belief in God and revelation to be felt so irresistibly as to make all considerations on the other side not reasons for doubt, but only difficulties to be answered or borne with. Another, looking at the facts in *his* own way, declares the reasons against dogmatic belief, which to his neighbour were but difficulties, to be final as against religious certainty. The question is, which of those two men is in such a frame of mind as to do justice to the question ? Which of them is in such a disposition of mind—supposing mere intellectual power to be equal—as to give the full and just weight to all considerations bearing on the matter, neither too much nor too little, and to be sensitive to all facts which should influence his decision one way or another ? and this question is to some extent considered by implication in my discussions, even when they profess to deal immediately with a narrower range of considerations than I am now supposing.

In conclusion I will say that I am quite conscious that there is very much more to be said on the subject than I have been able to include in the dialogues which follow ; but I hope that I have suggested a train of thought which should tend to show that the serious attitude of the religious mind has in it, on principles of the merest common sense, elements which are essential to the discovery of truth. Also I hope that in doing so I have incidentally shown that there are, also on principles of the merest common sense, grave defects in the sceptical attitude of mind; that it is naturally allied with great deficiencies in the higher intellectual qualities. It seems to exalt mere quickness in finding fault, and to depreciate the power of reaching out to fresh knowledge, which is surely in reality the intellect's greatest and highest office. In its extremest form it led Hume to deny the existence of any external reality beyond his own consciousness—which seems to be a *reductio ad absurdum* of a principle which makes complete analysis of reasons for belief the test and the only test of the belief's validity. The true view is surely Cardinal Newman's, that the mind sees more than it can explain, and that it is the single eye for truth and the keenness to find it which, as making us sensitive to all that should lead to it, really does lead to it in the long run, and in many cases assures us that truth is found. And with this disposition of mind the wish to believe is, as I have endeavoured to show, in many cases inseparably allied.

One final word as to the form I have adopted. My great aim has been to make Darlington, the sceptic, not a man of straw, but a real man, and to give an account, as true to nature as I am able, of such a discussion as might take place between two men of fairly equal abilities. It seems to me above all things important in these days to show that a Christian can fully realize the plausibleness of religious scepticism. None will have confidence in a remedy if it is plain that the disease is not understood by him who offers it. And again, if the picture is a successful likeness it vindicates for Christianity one great test of truth according to the saying of De Maistre, that "Truth can understand error, though error can never understand truth."

THE WISH TO BELIEVE.

graduate at Muriel College, Oxford, he had been thrown in contact with men of keen and eager mind, whose principal ambition it was to keep pace with what is called the thought of the day; and who had sufficient powers of argument to

c

THE WISH TO BELIEVE.

DIALOGUE I.

BERNARD DARLINGTON and Edmund
Ashley became acquainted for the first time
during their residence together for some ten days
at a small hotel near Lake Coniston on the
borders of Cumberland. They were men whose
calling and religious tenets would argue them to
be very dissimilar in character: but who had, in
reality, many sympathies in common. Darlington
was by profession a barrister. When an under-
graduate at Muriel College, Oxford, he had been
thrown in contact with men of keen and eager
mind, whose principal ambition it was to keep
pace with what is called the thought of the day ;
and who had sufficient powers of argument to

c

enable them to say a good deal that was difficult to answer in favour of advanced opinions on things in general, and on religion in particular. He had constantly heard those around him speak of the absurdity of expecting *certainty* on questions connected with another world, when all the arguments producible in favour of religious belief had by many of the very greatest minds been long since weighed in a balance and found wanting. This idea had been for many years a first principle with him, and seemed indeed only the veriest common sense. "Who am I," thought he, "that I should pretend to see clearly and conclusively the force of arguments which Hume and Gibbon, Huxley and Spencer have felt to be inconclusive?" Questions as to the immortality of the soul, the Divine origin of Christianity, and the like, should, he thought, be left alone by a sensible, rational man. The controversies in their regard might indeed have an historical interest, but no more. Dispassionate judges held them to be incapable of solution; and the idea of certainty in their regard had only arisen from the passionate craving which exists in some minds to have definite knowledge and

grounds for hope as to the future, which, in days
when emotion was strong and reason not very
circumspect, led many to catch at any theory,
however insufficiently proved, that professed to
satisfy their desire. Some great intellects of
mystical and ideal tendencies were led by this
same desire to create systems of belief which
should answer to the need of their own hearts,
and should at the same time serve as a sanction
for their moral code. To aid them in their
endeavour they had invoked those myths and
traditions of the past which in a more or less
confused way express the anticipations, hopes, and
fears of nations in the course of their history,
and the speculations of the popular mind; and
out of these raw materials of emotion, desire,
and tradition, supported by a certain measure of
plausible argument *à priori*, they constructed
their several religious theories. The mass of
mankind get their knowledge from the teaching
of experts, and when master minds professed
aloud their belief, the multitude felt that there
must be ample warrant for it, and hence it soon
spread; and as faith is in its very nature unquestioning, once gained, it was not readily

abandoned. Then, when religion in one shape or another had thus become considerably diffused, common consent seemed to be a confirmation of its truth. There was, moreover, much in the nature of the human mind and of the world in which we live to strengthen religious belief as soon as it had come into existence. Man's natural feeling of helplessness and dependence amid the powers of nature harmonised well with the account which had been given him of certain potent and invisible personalities having control over the universe; while the idea of prayer and of its efficacy in securing Divine protection was readily welcomed as lessening the feeling of impotent dread which must have arisen in the human mind, should these vast powers have been deemed to act blindly, and without regard to our own wishes or happiness.

Such was, Darlington considered, in outline the origin of all religions—from the systems of Moses, Zoroaster, and Buddha, to those of Christ and Mohammed—and the foundations on which they rested needed only to be looked at that it might appear how weak and unsubstantial they were. There might *very likely* be much

truth to be found as it were " in solution " among
the various creeds; but the idea of religious
certainty was, he said, " utterly incompatible with
exact thought; " a phrase, we may remark by the
way, which is often made to do duty for a great
deal of the thing which it signifies; which
magnificently condemns as unworthy of notice
many arguments which require for their refu-
tation considerably greater power of " exact
thought " than is possessed by him who disdain-
fully dismisses them. Darlington was, then,
what is commonly called an Agnostic, using the
word in its wider sense. He had been educated
without any deep concern about religious subjects,
and had believed rather because he never questioned himself about his belief than deeply or
after reflection; and therefore it had not cost
him much to abandon a Christianity which in
him had never amounted to much more than an
external profession.

Ashley was a Catholic priest; the Professor of
Moral Philosophy at Sandown College. He had
been a Catholic all his life, and had never been
touched by the wave of scepticism which is sweep-
ing over the non-Catholic world in England.

He had arrived at that time of life at which the opinions are generally fixed and set; so that now, although he might understand a point of view differing from his own by force of imagination, there was little fear of his own belief being in any way shaken. He had, however, great powers of sympathy, and was readily drawn to Darlington by the perception in him of a natural temperament both attractive in itself, and especially so to him by reason of its similarity to his own. Both of them had a strong love for scenery, which, in the Lake country, is a sure bond of union ; both were men of active minds and keen interests; and though one was by profession a dealer in syllogisms and the other a barrister, neither was given to that argumentativeness which so often makes clever men disagreeable. They conversed a great deal, but rather with a view to gaining information than to disputing. Religion was naturally a subject of interest to both ; to one as the great centre of the outgoing phase of civilised thought ; and to the other as the foundation of his whole life, and man's most important possession. Father Ashley found in his new acquaintance, in the course of their rows on the lake and

rambles among the hills, so much of natural
religious feeling, and so fair and candid a mind,
as to make him form great hopes that some day
or other he might come to a knowledge of the
truth. Rightly judging, however, that much
more than mere argument is required for conversion, he asked him to come and spend a few days
at Sandown after the students had reassembled at
the end of the vacation, in the hope that the
sight of the practical working of Catholicism and
its influence over the lives of the boys, so far as
these might be seen even by a casual visitor,
might arouse within him a still greater interest
in the subject, and spur him on to more active
inquiry. In the course of their conversations it
transpired that Walton, an old college friend of
Darlington's, and a convert to Catholicism, was
now a priest in the immediate neighbourhood of
the college. He had been driven by the free-
thinking spirit at Muriel in a direction exactly
opposite to his friend. Dismayed at seeing so
many cherished convictions, of whose truth he
was deeply conscious, called into question and
cleverly combated, he soon began to feel the
difficulty—nay, the impossibility—of holding to

the principle that each separate belief had to be proved by him on its own merits against men of far superior knowledge and logical *acumen*. He felt that life was not long enough for a work of this kind, and again he was often most dissatisfied with his own advocacy of the various dogmas. "Surely," he said to himself, "life is meant for action, and it cannot be right that the very foundations and springs of well-doing should be in constant danger of giving way. All my efforts are spent in securing *them*, and very insecurely after all. How can I go on doing good when at every step the very thoughts I rely upon as proving my course to be worth pursuing are cleverly attacked as being so many illusions, and when I feel my own knowledge to be in many cases so imperfect that I am ashamed to rest my belief on it?" This feeling led him by degrees to recognise the voice of God in the Catholic Church speaking absolutely and categorically, and relying not on processes of argument, but on its own Divine mission and inspiration. He recognised that the Church was God's vicegerent on earth. He had studied her in her various aspects, her moral and ascetical theology, her

official pronouncements, her practical system, and
he found in them all a profound knowledge of
human nature, and an uncompromising and
elevated moral tone quite unlike anything he
had seen elsewhere. He was not at all blind
to the human weakness of her members, or the
scandals of her history; but the system, and the
representatives of the system—those who had
taken full advantage of the assistance it offers
to mankind—gave to the Church in his eyes a
stamp of Divinity. *Vera incessu patuit dea.*
And when his mind had taken this step, he felt
that his old belief in the primary Christian truths
rested on a new and secure basis. It was no
longer his own reasonings from the nature of
things or from Scripture, but the voice of God
speaking through His chosen oracle which sanc-
tioned his creed; and this being recognised, the
mazes of human speculation were powerless to
mislead him any more. Indeed, when he had
once satisfied himself that he had found a living
guide and teacher, he considerably lost his intellectual interests, which had ever been concerned
more or less with inquiry into religious subjects,
and betook himself on his reception into the

Church to active missionary work as a priest. Darlington had been grieved at the very opposite courses he and his friend had taken. " You will never convince me, however, Walton," he said. " Your change is no argument to me, much as I believe in your ability. You were *determined* to believe; you were not dispassionate, so you are no fair judge. You wouldn't give up your pet ideas, though, if you had been really fair, you should have done so. Your wish to believe was father to your thought."

" I was determined to get at the *truth*," replied Walton. " I believed Christianity to be the truth, and I was resolved, if there was a way to seeing its truth more clearly, that I would find it ; and I *have* found it."

Darlington arrived at Sandown at about eight o'clock on a Thursday evening, some six weeks after the vacation had terminated. He was favourably impressed on entering the college, which was on a far larger scale than he was prepared for. The stone corridors, pointed arches, and Gothic windows and doors, gave it quite the appearance of a mediæval monastery. The professors had finished dinner when he arrived, but

Walton had been asked to meet him, and they
dined together with Ashley in the professors'
parlour, a spacious room, simply but tastefully
furnished with an oaken sideboard and chairs,
a large mantelpiece of carved stone, Pugin's
design, standing over the fireplace. After dinner
Ashley presented Darlington to the President,
who asked him if he would wish to attend
the benediction service which was about to
commence. He expressed his willingness, and
was ushered into the chapel, a small edifice built
in the Gothic style of the elder Pugin, and adorned
with much handsome carving in wood and stone.
He was a good deal struck by the serious and
earnest demeanour of the boys, both older and
younger. They all seemed, without any undue
affectation of fervour, to be quietly conscious that
they had a serious duty to perform, and to perform it as though they meant what they were
doing. At the end of the service one of Bishop
Challoner's solid and practical discourses was
read, as the subject for the next morning's meditation, and then all turned round to the statue of
Our Lady, which was so designed as to appear to
offer the prayers of those in the chapel at the

throne of grace, and sang the beautiful hymn,
" Maria, mater gratiæ, dulcis parens clementiæ,
tu nos ab hoste protege et mortis horâ suscipe."
After all was over, a certain number of the professors, principally the younger ones, adjourned
to the parlour to have tea, and invited Darlington
and Walton to join them there.

" Certainly," said Darlington to Father Davenport, the procurator, as they entered the parlour
together, " your liturgy and ritual are extremely
beautiful. I think the idea of devotion to the
Virgin Mother so touching. The ideal of a
tender mother with human affections, to whom
you have recourse as to one who can readily
understand you and sympathise with you in your
troubles, who has no heart to refuse to plead for
you and help you, is to me a most beautiful conception."

" And yet," said Father Davenport, " it is so
often a difficulty to outsiders ! It is one of the
commonest stumbling-blocks in the way of con-
versions."

" I think it very beautiful," pursued Darlington.
" I declare, when you all turned round to the
statue at the end of the prayers and sang that

hymn to the Virgin, the idea of trust and confidence in the invisible Mother who intercedes for you and protects you all, was so strongly expressed that it quite moved me—let me see, what are the words?"

Father Davenport repeated them. "Yes," continued Darlington, "with the two 'amens' at the end, one like the echo of the other. It affected me very much."

"Ah! my dear friend," said Ashley, who came into the room while he was speaking, "a man who has the soul to feel all that should be a Catholic. He is out of place anywhere but in the true Church."

Darlington smiled. "I am afraid a good deal more is wanted for my conversion than that," he said; "you would hardly have me *believe* in a doctrine simply because I think it beautiful and consoling?"

"No," said Father Ashley, "but a man who has insight into and perception of the Divine beauty of Catholic doctrine, must, I think, be on the high road to the perception of its *truth*. His admiration for it is surely a grace of the Holy Spirit, and if he is not unfaithful the rest will follow."

"Won't you sit down?" said Father Davenport. They had been standing while they were talking, and Darlington perceived on looking round that the other professors were gradually settling themselves down in knots of two or three at different parts of the long table. Walton was seated at a little distance from them, intent on something in a newspaper. Darlington and Ashley sat down.

"Let me give you a cup of tea, Mr. Darlington," said Father Davenport; "we are rather proud of our tea and our cream too."

"I shall be very glad to try it," replied Darlington. "I think that good tea is the most refreshing drink that ever was invented. No sugar, thanks. Of course," he continued to Ashley, "you express the thing differently from me, but I think we mean pretty much the same thing, and you are not the first man whom I have heard talk in a similar way. That manner of speaking and thinking, which I perceive in so many religious people, as though the fact that a doctrine is consoling makes it also true, is, I think, at the root of a good deal of my scepticism. It makes me suspect the whole basis of their belief."

"But I think you are wrong," said Ashley. "We may say that the intrinsic beauty of a doctrine is an *additional* sign that it comes from God, but none would maintain that all doctrines which are beautiful are true. Take the Pagan myths; many of them were the creations of highly poetic minds; but certainly none of us believe in Elysian fields, however pleasant a prospect they might be."

"Perhaps I expressed myself too generally," said Darlington. "I don't suppose that Christians would expressly *maintain* that a doctrine which is beautiful is therefore true. But still I must say that all my observations have tended to convince me that in very many cases their real state of mind falls very little short of that. They have *some* additional reasons, no doubt, but very insufficient ones; and their chief motive for believing is because belief is consoling and desirable. Do you remember Gibbon's account of the belief of the Christians of Rome under Pope Gregory the Great? He says that their temporal dangers and misfortunes, from the constant invasions of the Lombard and various other causes, led them to lend a ready ear to the

hopes which the preacher held out to them of a
happier state of things beyond the grave. Well,
it seems to me that this is the state of many
now-a-days. They are not happy in this world,
and so they readily believe on very insufficient
evidence tidings of another and a more satisfactory future life, and doctrines connected with
it which tend to console them."

"Should you say that the doctrine of hell
tended to comfort or console?" put in a youngish
man who had been listening to the conversation.

Darlington hesitated. "It is not fair," he
said, "to isolate a doctrine from the system to
which it belongs. It is almost proverbial that
hope, even though one pays for it with a certain
measure of fear, is preferable to a dead level of
hopeless dulness. I don't think you can dispute
that the Christian view of the world, *taken as a
whole,* giving as it does a *greatness* to life and a
connection with a realised ideal, imparting to
labour and privation, and all that would naturally
be irksome, a value which far more than compen-
sates for their unpleasantness, and holding out a
hope for the gratification in the future of all
our highest and deepest yearnings, is, in spite of

everything on the other side, a far preferable
and more consoling one to a mind which is dissatisfied with the present, than the prospect of
dull repetition of past experiences until, in the
end, annihilation arrives."

"Surely," said Father Ashley, going back to
the first question which Darlington had raised,
"you cannot apply Gibbon's remark to the present age or to this country. He spoke of an
exceptional state of things when the Romans
were so wretched that they were ready to cling
to any idea which afforded them a ray of hope.
Not that I admit Gibbon's charge even with
reference to the Romans, but I think there is
even less colour for it now-a-days."

"The exact circumstances may be different,"
replied Darlington, "but the general fact remains
the same. Dissatisfaction was no doubt more
widely spread then. But in one shape or another
the *wish* to believe seems to me to be at the root
of all religion still. One man turns to religion
because he is *ennuyé* with the world; another
clings to it because he has been brought up to it,
and it is bound up closely with all the memories
and associations of his childhood; another is

D

attached to his creed because his ancestors died for it.   Many become Roman Catholics because of the effect the gorgeous vestments, incense, and tapers have upon them.   Newman himself admits that many can give no better account of the matter than that the Catholic religion is true because its fragrance is as perceptible to their moral sense as that of flowers to their sense of smell. In all these cases religion or a particular form of religion is embraced or adhered to from no rational motive, but simply because the believer wants to believe.   As I said, the wish is father to the thought.   Look at Moody and Sankey's converts—even the best of them.   They had no new reason given them for belief.   They were pleased and excited by the hymns and sermons. Sankey's performances on the harmonium constituted one of their chief motives.   Religious belief gave them under the circumstances pleasant excitement, and so they believed—not because their intellects had received any new light — but because what they saw and heard made them *wish* to believe.   I have seen so much of this that I am on my guard.   *I* am quite alive to the consoling power of religion.   I often suffer from

great depression of spirits and *tædium vitæ.* I
remember a schoolfellow of mine of a melancholy
disposition, who used to go about crying out,
'Who will tell me of something to look forward to?' That is often my own feeling, and
religious conviction would be the greatest comfort to me. But I am so alive to the fallacy of
religious minds—the fallacy of believing because
one *wishes* to believe—that I myself can never
be a believer."

"Don't you think, Mr. Darlington," said the
young man who had spoken before, "that the
strong wish implanted in man's nature for religion
may be worth something as an *argument?* Most
of our appetites and cravings have a legitimate
satisfaction; their existence seems to point to the
existence of an object capable of satisfying them.
Hunger is correlative with food, love with objects
of love, and so forth; so it seems hard to believe
that man has a thirst for religious knowledge,
and yet that such knowledge is entirely unattainable."

" I don't think," replied Darlington, "that you
are attacking exactly the position I have assumed,
though doubtless I do tend to think religious

certainty incapable of attainment. I do not
speak of any natural or general craving for
religion among mankind. What I say is that
attachment to religion or to a particular form of
religion on the part of an individual, and for
reasons peculiar to his case, so often supersedes
—and most unreasonably supersedes—argument.
This would hold good even if I granted what you
are saying. I am speaking merely of that common fallacy—believing what suits one, or is
pleasant—creeping into religious inquiry."

"I don't yet see," said Ashley, "how you *prove*
that the wish of the believer *is* father to his
thoughts. After one has arrived by reason and
grace at doctrines which are consoling, one may
feel that they *are* consoling; but that is no proof
that it is their consoling power which has made
one believe them. If it is proved to me beyond
doubt that I have come into a fortune of £10,000
a year, I may find the fact very consoling, but it
would be very unjust in you to turn round on me
and tell me that I believe it simply because it is
consoling."

"I really could not give you in mood and figure
an exact proof that it is as I say," said Darlington.

" It is a matter of observation rather than of argument; and then, every one knows the tendency of human nature to believe what is pleasant. I think that it is at least a very remarkable fact that, whereas the evidences of Christianity are, to a great extent, common property and in everybody's hands, the people who are convinced by them are those who have what is called religious minds, or, in other words, who wish to believe. Lacordaire points out somewhere that, whereas Fénelon found in Scripture the strongest evidence of the truth of Christianity, Voltaire found in it only food for laughter. The proofs, such as they were, were open to both alike; but to him who had no prepossession in favour of belief they were quite insufficient. Take Hume and Johnson, again; both able men and capable of doing justice to the arguments on both sides. Hume was dispassionate and unprejudiced; Johnson had, as one sees at every turn in his life, strong emotional religious cravings. The calm and dispassionate man found the evidences for Christianity quite insufficient—and surely such a man is the best judge of their *true* worth. It is the same now-a-days: your calm, clearheaded men of science think them quite insufficient and fallacious."

" I don't know that calm and unbiassed men are always the best judges," said Father Ashley. " No doubt bias is a bad thing, but I think that apathy is worse. If your unprejudiced men are apathetic, if their minds and hearts are in things other than religion, I had rather have a *prejudiced* man who is in earnest, and whose heart is in the matter. If I were a prisoner, I had rather my judge were somewhat prejudiced against me, than that he had neither bias nor sense of responsibility. The former kind of judge, if he is conscientious, has something in him that one can appeal to which may overcome his prejudice ; the latter may condemn me through mere sleepiness or inattentiveness. You may reason away prejudice, but not apathy, as its very characteristic is that it takes no pains to attend to your reasonings."

Here a man, who had been an attentive listener for the last five minutes, but had not as yet spoken, broke into the conversation. He was somewhat stout, of middle age, and spoke with a resonant bass voice. He had been sitting alone at the other side of the table with a newspaper before him, but had for some time been making small pretence of reading it, as the conversation was evidently engrossing his attention. This was Father Walton, of whom we have already spoken.

"I think, Darlington," he said, "that your philosophy is at fault. You speak of the well-known tendency of human nature to believe what is pleasant. Well, I should say not only that such a tendency is not well known, but that it does not exist at all. I think the truth is exactly the opposite. If I am very anxious that a thing should be true, I find that I am slower, and not quicker, in believing it."

The others seemed to be waiting for him to explain himself.

"For instance," he continued, "many years ago I was weak enough to bet rather heavily on a horse which was running in the Derby. When the first report got out that that horse had won, I found that all my companions, who were not betting men, believed it at once; but I was not satisfied until I had seen it in print, and its truth was beyond the possibility of doubt. Yet I was

far more anxious than the others that the report
should prove true."

"That does certainly seem to be an exception
to the rule," said Darlington. "But still you
can't deny that, *as a rule*, men tend to believe
what is pleasant. 'Thy wish was father, Harry,
to that thought,' has passed into a proverb."

"I can't admit that it *is* a rule," replied
Walton. "When boys here are anxious for a
holiday, and have sent to ask the President to
give one, I don't at all find that they over-esti-
mate the reasons in favour of expecting it. The
other day, in a French religious community where
I was staying, they were electing a new superior,
and I found many who expected their favourite
candidate to fail, though there was really a good
chance in his favour. It seems to me that there
is no rule of the kind you suppose."

Here Father Davenport interrupted the conversation for a moment to replenish Darlington's
cup with tea. Ashley, however, took the question up. Much as he wished to convince his
friend, he could not see his way to accepting
Walton's uncompromising denial of the former's
principle.

"Surely you will not dispute, Walton," he said, "that there is a class of cases on the other side. I remember a very eminent physician who was so determined to believe that his remedies were effective, that if you told him they had not cured you, he simply answered that you were wrong and that they *must* have done so. It used to be quite an amusing scene with poor Bowring, whom you remember. Bowring suffered from very severe headaches, and Dr. R——, as I will call him (for I don't want to mention his name), was confident that he could cure him in two days. At the expiration of that time Dr. R—— made his appearance, and said with a confident smile, 'Well, and how are the headaches *now*?' 'As bad as ever,' replied Bowring. 'Ah, then,' said Dr. R—— quite gravely, 'you did not take my prescriptions.' 'I took them most religiously,' said Bowring. 'Oh!' said the doctor in a tone of relief, 'then the headaches have gone.' 'But they haven't! I feel them still,' said poor Bowring. 'No, no,' said R——, 'believe me, they are gone. You have had so much of them that you can't help imagining that they are there still, but I assure you they are gone;' and it was impossible to convince him that they were not. Bowring had to pay his guinea for nothing, and to go to another doctor."[1]

Every one laughed. "Poor Bowring!" said Father Davenport, who had been listening to the story. "I can well imagine his distress of mind. I suspect he found food for a fortnight's grumbling in it."

"Well," continued Ashley, "I think *that* a strong case of believing because one wishes to believe. Dr. R——— had made up his mind that his medicine was to be successful, and therefore he would have it that it *had* been."

"I remember a case something like that," said Darlington, "of old Mrs. Arton, the wife of one of our farmers in Yorkshire. She had manufactured some ointment which she believed to be an infallible remedy for bruises and sores of every kind. To the best of my belief it really retarded their cure very considerably. However, in the end nature's tendency to self-healing used to assert itself, and it was most amusing to see the

[1] All the anecdotes in this paper are substantially true, although reference to persons and places has been carefully avoided. Of course, their value as illustrations *depends* on their being true.

old lady's triumph at the complete success of her ointment."

"I suppose," said Ashley, "she argued, 'post hoc, propter hoc.' The cure was subsequent to the anointing, therefore it was due to it."

"It was just the same," continued Darlington, "with her prophecies about the weather. They were invariably wrong, but this never in the least shook her faith in her own powers; and when a glorious, still, sunny day appeared after she had prophesied 'heavy rain and high winds,' she would gravely assure you that it was raining in some parts."

"Surely," said the young man who had spoken before, "the belief of some of the Tichborne tenants in the claimant illustrates what you are saying, Mr. Darlington. I should think there is little doubt that their strong wish to see their squire back again had a great influence in determining their belief."

"Or," added Ashley, "take a conceited coxcomb, who thinks all the world is admiring him. That surely comes from his love of admiration."

"I don't think we want for instances," said Darlington; "you must admit, Walton, that men have, at least in many cases, and under certain circumstances, a tendency to believe what is pleasant on very insufficient evidence."

" I admit," replied Walton, " that men often deceive themselves into *thinking* what is pleasant, where there is no danger of being brought immediately face to face with the fact that it is untrue ; but I don't think that in those cases they seriously *believe*, though they may say they do. If they have the pleasure of the thought without the pain of finding out that it is untrue, it gives them for the time almost as much satisfaction as real and deep belief. But it is not belief—or at least it is not conviction."

" Dear me," suddenly interrupted Ashley, " what a very animated conversation is going on between Merton, Kershaw, and Gordon Brabourne ! I suppose it is their usual topic— Roman *versus* Gothic in architecture and vestments."

" He doesn't mean what he says, Gordon," Merton was saying, a man with lively manner and pleasant voice, who sat at the end of the table. " If the Romans wore the present Gothic vestments, and the square ones were Gothic,

Kershaw would see all sorts of defects in the square ones, and would discover all manner of hidden devotional and symbolical meaning in the many-folded robes so much loved by Pugin. Now, don't protest. You hold that the Roman Pontiff's infallibility extends to the shape of your *antipendium*, the carving on your pillars, and the cut of your albs ; you know you do."

"Kershaw is a recent convert," explained Ashley to Darlington ; "a splendid fellow, but a little extreme. He has just come back from Rome, and Merton chaffs him about what he calls his Roman fever."

"My dear Merton," replied Kershaw, "how can you talk so much at random? Whoever said it was a question of infallibility ? All that I say is, that where Rome has set the example our duty is not to criticise but to imitate ; that we do better by trying to appreciate duly the customs and usages of Holy Church, and to admire them as they deserve, than by setting up idols of our own creation in opposition."

"Rank heresy, Kershaw," said Merton. "As though the style of architecture in Rome were set up for our imitation, any more than the way the

Romans cut their hair, or the shape in which they trim their beards."

"It seems to me," said Brabourne, the third speaker, "that if you insist on tracing these things to their origin, and making them more than a mere matter of taste, you should not forget that the present Roman architecture is originally Pagan—an introduction of the Renaissance. Gothic is the creation of Christianity."

"Besides," continued Merton, "Kershaw is not even content with making it simply a question of what is authoritatively held up for our *imitation.* He demands *interior assent* also. Roman architecture and vestments are not only to be *used* by every loyal son of the Church, but to be *admired* also. The duty of interior assent is not confined to decisions on faith and morals; matters of taste are likewise infallibly decided for us."

"You are very hard on me, Merton," replied Kershaw; "I never said that anything had been infallibly decided. I spoke only of my own taste in the matter, and it was you that insisted that it was grounded on the teaching of Rome; though I certainly do think that a priest shows a more becoming and loyal spirit if he is not content with obeying simply the letter of the law, but tries likewise to admire and like what Mother Church tells us to make use of, instead of looking in the first place to find out what he can criticise and run down without fear of formal heresy."

"Without fear of formal heresy!" repeated Merton; "what Mother Church *tells* us to make use of. Good heavens! I suppose you would agree with Ashburton; Ashburton, after he had been to Rome (shortly after his conversion), on his return to England used frequently to bring into church with him two large dogs with bells attached to their collars, which ran about during mass, making a most unearthly noise, because it reminded him of Rome."

"I am surprised the congregation allowed it," said Brabourne.

"It was a very small congregation," said Merton, "and he was a considerable personage there, and a great benefactor to the mission, so he was privileged. I remember asking him what he did it for, and he gravely assured me that it had a most devotional effect upon him."

"Nonsense!" said Brabourne.

"He did really," said Merton. "I suggested an idea which would make what he said more rational. I said I supposed that all that reminded him of Rome was so associated in his mind with his first fervour, that it had a great attraction for him. But he would not accept this explanation at all. He would have it that there was something in its own nature devotional in the sound of the collar bells of these animals as they ran about in the church."

Every one laughed except Kershaw, who said, "Well, if you are going to make a joke of the whole subject, I don't think I can do much good by arguing it out with you. Besides, I have to say the half-past five o'clock mass to-morrow for the servants, so I will wish every one goodnight."

"I don't think he was sorry of an excuse to get away," said Brabourne, as Kershaw left the room. "He knows that when he gets on these subjects he has to fight against considerable odds; and then you are always so merciless with him, Merton."

"Yes," put in Ashley, from the other end of the table, "you are really too hard on him,

Merton. Remember, Newman lays it down as one of the marks of a well-bred man that he is merciful to the absurd."

" Well, I really think it does him good," said Merton. " I have no patience with men who talk as though the cut of your chasuble and the length of your cotta were matters authoritatively ruled by the Holy See. As though great Rome, who is so large-hearted and liberal wherever she can be so without compromising principle, who tolerates an Armenian and a Greek rite utterly unlike her own, would ever indulge in such petty tyranny over our artistic tastes."

" Kershaw will be a very different man ten years hence," said Brabourne. " Some converts are so determined to find ideal perfection in every stick and stone in Rome that their judgment as to things Roman is completely warped."

" To me," said Ashley, " there is something admirable in Kershaw's spirit, though I should not go the length he does. ' Love me, love my dog,' says the proverb. I think it shows true devotion to Rome to have an affection for all, even the smallest things, that remind one of her."

" Yes," said Merton, " but the proverb does

E

not say 'Believe in me, believe my dog to be perfect,' or ' Condemn others for not believing it to be perfect.' "

" Surely," said Darlington, turning to Ashley and Walton, " Mr. Kershaw's frame of mind, as you describe it, is another instance of the very thing we have been talking about. His wish to find ideal perfection in everything Roman makes him think he has found it."

" I remember," said Brabourne, " an amusing instance of the same sort of thing when I took Compton—the Muriel man who was received two years ago—to Rome, just after his conversion. He had such an intense belief in the all-pervading piety of the place, that he gave a religious inter- pretation to everything he saw. We were stroll- ing one day in the Campagna and lost our way. We wanted to find the Flaminian gate, and so we asked an old carter whom we met which was our way. He looked a surly old fellow, and either found a difficulty in understanding our bad Italian, or did not feel in the humour for conver- sation. At any rate, not one word could we get out of him. I began saying, ' What a grumpy old man that is !' but Compton was quite indig-

nant with me for my shallow and uncatholic
view of the matter. 'This comes,' he said, 'of
living in a Protestant country, where all motives
are secular and natural. Depend upon it, that
man is under a vow of silence undertaken in
expiation for some sin of the tongue.'"

"Well, I remember our friend Kershaw here
used to talk," said Merton, "as though all the
actions of a Roman were religious in object and
motive, until at last I asked him point blank if
he supposed that every man, woman, and child
in Rome was a person of interior life, and he
was quite offended at my making a joke of it.
'I am sure they are,' he said."

"Well now," said Darlington, "after all you
have told us, Mr. Merton, you should be a good
authority on the question we have just been discussing. Don't you think that in a general way
a man is more ready to believe in a thing because
he wishes it to be so?"

"You mean, I suppose," said Merton, "that
men like Kershaw believe Roman vestments to be
perfect because they are determined to find everything that is Roman perfect?"

"Well, it seems to me from what you have

been saying," said Darlington, "that men of this stamp have made up their minds to find their ideal realised when they enter the Church. They are sick of constant contention and are enamoured of the idea of an authority which they are to reverence as infallible, which is to be decisive, and to set all fruitless disputation at rest. And then they expect her to fulfil more than she ever could fulfil or has promised—to decide on matters which she has neither the power nor the will to decide on; and with this expectation in their minds they see in the customs of Rome— which are merely *private* customs—the decisions of authority."

"They follow Rome in matters in which she acts, so to speak, as a private person, and not officially," said Merton, who was more intent upon the peculiarities of Kershaw than upon the application Darlington was making of them. "They remind me of those who imitate the mannerisms of a great man as though his very imperfections must have a touch of his Divine genius. They are like the actors who imitate Irving's way of walking and articulating, whereas most sensible men know that these are, to say the least, not at all essential to his greatness as an actor."

"I can't help admiring it," said Ashley. "It is devotion of the intensest sort which loves even the most insignificant thing connected with its object."

"I can't agree," said Darlington. "I think it is ten to one that such a mind is a small one, and loves *only* what is unimportant; that it is incapable of appreciating true greatness. The actor who takes most note of Irving's gait and voice will not be his most intelligent admirer. A greater mind will take no note of them, but will pass to the *soul* of his acting. It is the small mind that observes his peculiarities, and ten to one stops short at *them*, and fails to appreciate anything beyond."

Merton and Brabourne here looked at their watches, and, finding that it was late, wished the others good-night and left the room.

"At any rate," resumed Darlington, "it seems pretty clear that the converts of whom we speak supply us with an illustration of the principle I was supporting. Here are men maintaining in opposition to the arguments of those who have

the very best right to speak, that all Rome's
ecclesiastical customs are perfection even from
an artistic point of view, and are designed as
models for the rest of the Church; and all this
simply because they have made up their minds
beforehand to find Rome all perfect."

"I think," said Ashley, "that both their expectation and their belief arise from a naturally
sanguine disposition. That seems to me the
solution of the whole difficulty we raised. It is
a matter of temperament; a sanguine man is
ready, a despondent man slow, to believe what
he wishes. Ask Father McArton yonder" (pointing to a grave-looking priest who was reading a
book and had taken no share in the conversation) "if he believes that Macmillan will publish
his translation of the Eclogues. He is very
anxious to think that he will, but he is not at
all a cheerful man, and I don't think you will
find him very *ready* to believe it."

Here Walton, who had for some time been
occupied with his own thoughts, interposed.
"Temperament has its effect, no doubt; but it
is a very imperfect account to give of the matter
to say that is *all*. A man may be ever so

sanguine, and yet in the case I gave before of
his having a large bet on a horse at the Derby,
he won't be over ready to believe on slight
evidence that he has won. On the other hand,
there may be far stronger reasons against the
truth of the coxcomb's high opinion of himself,
and yet he won't give it up. The coxcomb is
not *honest* with himself. He nurses the pleasure
of his vanity; and as there is no external test, as
he is not forced to verify or disprove the truth of
his view, he is able to keep it. The man who
has the bet, on the contrary, is forced by the
circumstances of the case to be honest with himself. He knows that the truth of his belief will
soon be tested. He will soon know whether it is
right or wrong, and there is little pleasure in the
mere expectation, if after all it proves wrong."

"This seems to me to be a new point," said
Darlington, "and I don't quite follow you."

"Well," said Walton, "I have been trying
while you were talking to see the essential distinction between the cases that have been cited
on both sides. I fancy I can point it out by an
example which has occurred to me, which I
think you will admit to be true to nature. There

are two very different states of mind—anxiety that something should be really true, and the wish to have the pleasure of believing something. Here are two pictures. First take some lazy, comfort-loving, and selfish man. He is walking with a companion on a sea beach. No one is visible near him. Suddenly he hears what he takes to be the shriek of a drowning man, beyond some rocks at the end of the beach. His companion thinks it is only children at play. The rocks are hard to climb, and at some distance off. The man is readily persuaded that it *is* only children at play, and that there is no call on him to climb the rocks, or assist anybody. There is one attitude of mind—one picture. Now for another. An affectionate mother is placed in exactly the same circumstances as my lazy man. She thinks she recognises in the shriek her son's voice. Her companion says it is only children at play; but this *does not satisfy her.* She entreats him to help her to climb the rocks, and they arrive just in time to rescue her son—for it is her son—from drowning. Now surely you won't deny that the mother would be far more desirous to be convinced that her son

was not drowning than the lazy man in the
parallel case;[1] yet her wish, far from making
her believe it, only makes her take all the more
pains to satisfy herself as to the true state of the
case. Genuine conviction that the fact is really
as she hoped is what she wants; and wishing for
it doesn't help her a bit to get it. Our other
friend, on the contrary, was not really and truly
anxious to ascertain the *fact.* He wished to
banish an unpleasant idea from his mind. I
don't think he was truly or deeply convinced
that there was no call on him to climb the
rocks. He was not anxious to be *convinced* that
there was no call; he only cared to *think* that
there was none. He did not wish to *adjust his
mind to the fact* at all; he only wished to have a
comfortable *idea,* and to banish an uncomfort-
able suspicion. He was not anxious that the

---

[1] A friend to whom I showed these pages objects that the
illustration is not apposite, as the mother's prompt response to
what she takes for her son's cry for help is instinctive, and so
affords no guarantee for the action of one who has not the
mother's instinct, under similar circumstances. I have, however, retained it, as I cannot myself see that the mother's action
is, strictly speaking, instinctive. Let those, however, who think
that it is so substitute for the mother a very affectionate friend,
and judge for themselves whether in that case also Walton's
picture is not true to nature.

fact should be as he wished; if he had been he would have used every means to ascertain whether it were so or not. If it is a matter of some thousands to a man that Oxford should have won the boat-race, he is not ready to believe it on slight evidence; on the contrary, he examines into the reports he hears far more carefully than another."

All listened attentively to Walton's explanation, and most felt that he had thrown light on the subject. There was a pause before Ashley said—

"Don't you think that in the case you have given the fact that there is an immediate prospect of the belief being verified, and again the fact that it is a question of *immediate action,* may affect the frame of mind of the individuals concerned? Of course in religious belief the case is otherwise. One has to wait for verification until the end of one's life."

"The only effect that I can see," said Walton, "is that it insures a person's being honest with himself. Where there is *no* immediate prospect of verification he can enjoy the luxury of a false belief without danger of discovery. Where there

is an immediate prospect he feels it is of no use
to think of anything but truth. If you observe,
my lazy man, who was *dishonest* with himself
and shirked his duty, took care that there should
be *no* immediate test of the truth of his thought.
Had he expected such a test, I think he would
have climbed the rocks and made sure of the
facts."

"Then," said Darlington slowly, "as I understand you, you hold that where there is a real
anxiety and wish about the *thing*—an honest
desire for the truth of the *thing*, and not merely
for the pleasure of the *thought*—that desire
makes you *less* ready rather than more ready
to believe."

"Precisely," said Walton; "a shallow self-
deceitful thought, called only by a misnomer
'belief,' may well enough be the result of wishing to believe; but true conviction never. I
remember well a lady of my acquaintance who
used to think her nephew a perfect paragon of
perfection, and far the cleverest man at his
college at Oxford. She sucked in eagerly all
the civil things that people said in his favour,
and systematically disbelieved less flattering

reports. Here was one sort of belief. It arose from her wish—but her wish for what? That her nephew should *really* be the cleverest and most successful man ? "

"I suppose so," said Ashley unguardedly.

"Not entirely so, I think," said Walton; "but mainly from her wish for the *satisfaction of thinking* that he was so. The actual fact was of secondary importance to her; but it is of primary importance to him who wants a real and deep conviction. I remember, too, in that very case that the truth of this was evidenced in a most amusing manner when this brilliant nephew was trying for a fellowship which was of some consequence to him. She paid far more attention to and was rendered far more anxious by arguments against the probability of his success, and seemed very doubtful as to the result—quite prepared for his failure; and why? Because *here* it was the *fact* of his success which was of moment, and not the pleasure of her own subjective impression."

"You are getting dreadfully metaphysical," said Darlington, laughing.

"I admit then," continued Walton, "that

where the satisfaction of believing a thing is what is desired, and the correspondence of your belief with objective fact is a matter of small anxiety or importance to yourself, the wish is often father to the thought. Belief is readily obtained, although its quality is extremely bad. But where the truth of the *fact* is of the first importance, and an untrue belief is useless; where *genuine conviction* of the fact in question is desired, the desire will not beget readiness but rather caution in believing. It will make a man less easily convinced than another by the evidence ready to hand. He so much wishes that the thing should be true that he fears to believe it, holding, in the words of the proverb, that it is 'too good to be true.' But, on the other hand, he is more ready than another to give himself every chance of discovering whether what he so much wishes for *be* really true. He is interested in the subject, and his desire will make him search for a road to certainty, instead of waiting until such a road is unmistakably pointed out to him. The wish then, as I have said, may be father to a shallow self-deceitful *idea*, but it renders *true conviction* in a certain sense (as I have explained) slower, although proportionally deeper and surer."

Here, for a time at least, Walton's homily came to a halt; and Darlington, who had been much interested with what he said, though a little bored at the argumentativeness and seriousness of his tone, continued turning over in his mind the whole question, and trying to put into shape his own impressions as to how much of truth there was in his friend's view.

"I don't deny," he said, as he absently stirred his empty teacup with his spoon, "that there is some truth in what you say. But as applied to religion it has a fallacy, and you know that Tennyson says that 'a lie which is half a truth is ever the blackest of lies.' You have to take it for granted that religious believers have these *deep convictions* and this *anxiety for truth*, and are not satisfied with prejudice. Of course the very thing I should say is that they are prejudiced and unfair. They view all the evidence partially. They ignore half of it."

"Well, of course," replied Walton, "I can't *prove* to you that they are unprejudiced. All I am saying is that if they are honest and anxious for true conviction—anxious about the fact of religious truth with all its consequences, and not only for its consoling power as a beautiful thought, then their anxiety to believe is no argument against them, but rather in their favour. Of course how far one is honest and convinced is a question which each man must answer from his own personal consciousness. I can't prove to another that I am deeply convinced, though I may be certain of it in my own mind."

" I suppose it comes to this," said Darlington, " that all your party are honest, and sincere, and convinced, and the rest, and all others are prejudiced and insincere. This is, to say the least, a decided and marked division of the human race."

" No, my dear Darlington," replied Walton, "you quite misunderstand me. My position in all that I am saying is purely negative. I am only answering your objection. All that I say is that where one is conscious of real conviction, one need not be afraid that it is the result of a wish to believe; and this because a desire to be convinced of a truth makes one harder and not easier of belief. I am defending our side of the question and not attacking you. There may be

prejudiced Christians who arrive at the truth in
a wrong way, or others who do not deeply believe.
All I say is, that if I am conscious of conviction,
I am sure it has not been caused by my wish to
believe."

Darlington was somewhat annoyed at a new
element he thought he perceived in the discussion.
His friend was not content with differing from
him intellectually; he seemed to impugn his
honesty and sincerity. His annoyance made him
lose the thread of the discussion.

"It comes to this," he said. " You feel convinced, *ergo* you are right. What do you say if
I reply, ' I am convinced that certainty on these
religious questions is impossible; that they are
outside our ken altogether; *ergo* I am right, and
it is so.' I have just as much right as you to lay
down the law. You make your own mind the
measure of all truth."

" You persist in misunderstanding me," said
Walton. "I allow as much to you as I do to
myself. If you feel really *sure* that religious certainty is unattainable, I think that a strong proof
that your belief is not the result of a wish to
think it so; and that is all that I say in my own

case. You tried to make out that one's wishes, so far as they influenced conviction, did so unreasonably; and in self-defence I tried to show that anxiety for certainty that something is true, is an assistance in learning the true state of the case; and that it spurs one on to search for whatever proofs on the subject are attainable; and that, far from making one's views of *existing* proofs sanguine, it has the contrary effect. Lastly, I maintain that where belief is the result of prejudice, there is generally a feeling that it is not firm or deeply rooted. The mind is dimly conscious of its own want of candour, and of not having done justice to the question; although, of course, explicit self-examination on the subject would be contrary to the very nature of an uncandid mind."

As Darlington made no reply, Walton pursued his own train of thought.

"I have always thought," he said, "that the shallowness of false and spurious convictions is excellently shown by Newman in quite a different connection in his *Essay on Assent.* He speaks of the confident opinions many people profess as to St. Paul's meaning in a particular text; and then

F

he supposes that St. Paul were suddenly to appear to answer for himself. How each speaker would modify and explain away what he had just been dogmatically asserting! Yet they had really persuaded themselves that their convictions were genuine, until there was a prospect of their being put to the test. When that prospect came, they were exposed to themselves and to others. As long as truth was not of the first moment to them, they tortured their minds into believing what prejudice or fancy dictated; or at best they professed certainty on most inadequate grounds, and where there was in reality no certainty. Their search had been not for truth, but for arguments to support their pet notions. They did not attempt to conform their minds honestly to the evidence before them, but viewed that evidence through the refracting medium of their own preconceived ideas, and gave all their real *effort* to the search for *arguments* in support of their views. Then suddenly, when truth became everything, and its discovery threatened to render impossible the satisfaction of believing and defending their own prejudices, the shallowness and unreality of their previous pretended convictions became unmistakable. It is the realizing that truth is everything, and the mere repose of believing what is pleasant (if after all the belief is wrong) *nothing*, that makes a conviction worthy of the name, and ensures its being genuine; and surely, as far as it goes, this state of mind renders it more probable that your belief is *right*. It is not believing a thing that makes it true, but the thing being true is all that gives any value to belief. One should realize this. ' If Christ be not risen again, your faith is vain.' These words always strengthen my faith. They show that the Apostle's absolute belief and intense enthusiasm did not make him forget that they rested, not on themselves, but on objective facts for support, and that if these facts were mistaken all was in vain. His conviction must have had deep root to stand against this thought. He felt that he had staked everything on his belief, and so no one could be more desirous for real certainty of its truth than he. Yet he so clearly realized that it was not the present satisfaction of believing, but the truth of what he believed that was important, that his desire and anxiety to be convinced was a guarantee of the depth of his conviction rather than a reason for suspecting it; and it seems to me that the case is the same with any earnest Christian who has a sense of realities. Of course he is anxious to convince himself; but he knows that a spurious conviction is worthless, and so his anxiety makes him all the more careful in the matter, lest he may be staking his all on an uncertainty."

Walton was evidently full of his subject, but his whole tone was out of sympathy with the bent of Darlington's mind, and the latter began to find it hard to bear an active part in the conversation. His friend was so changed. He spoke with such earnestness—unpleasant earnestness. It seemed a sort of reproach to Darlington for being unable to rise to the same pitch. Then all his language about " depth of conviction " and the " necessity of being in earnest " was so new. Talking to him was a strong contrast to the religious discussions he remembered at Muriel years ago. They had been so delightful. Every one interested in the subject; no one unpleasantly excited or anxious: theory after theory mooted, discussed, and criticised; a real intellectual treat. Even to-night they had had a pleasant talk enough until Walton had absorbed the lion's share of the conversation. He introduced a tone of his own. It was like the change from fencing with foils to a duel with rapiers. He seemed to talk not for pleasure but like one who is defending something personal of great value, which he fears may be taken from him. At Muriel an objection used to be welcomed as fresh food for discussion; but with Walton it seemed to hurt and distress him. His answers were wanting in brightness. They were painfully elaborate and full. He seemed never content until he had pushed his arguments as far as possible, and answered objections to the very utmost that they admitted. In short his tone and manner had commenced to bore Darlington. Ashley was very quick to observe this, and he feared that the good effect of the conversation on Darlington might be undone if it was prolonged. As he saw that Walton was preparing to continue in the same strain, he said, "I think it is getting too late for so exciting a discussion, and you will not sleep, Father Walton, if you go any deeper into metaphysics and psychology." Walton looked up and saw in Darlington's face the true state of the case.

"I fear I have been too warm," he said, "but that is the natural consequence of the subject we have been discussing. Dr. Johnson says that the reason the early Greeks could argue so good-humouredly about religion was because they did not believe in it."

The conversation passed to indifferent topics, and Darlington was thankful for the relief. Walton was obliged to go some ten minutes later, and his departure was the signal for the retirement of those who had not as yet gone to bed; and as Darlington was tired after his journey, he was not sorry to follow suit and make his way to his room. Ashley saw his friend upstairs and wished him good-night, leaving him hardly in the humour to ask himself candidly how far his own views had been affected by what he had heard. The chief impression left on his mind by the conversation was that it had tired him at the end of a tiring day. But the seed was sown in his mind, and doubtless was destined one day to issue in fruit of some kind.

DIALOGUE II.

DARLINGTON passed a night of unbroken rest and was awakened at six o'clock on Friday morning by a gong, which seemed to him to sound just outside his room, and then to make its way along the winding passages, echoing more and more faintly in the distance. This he rightly concluded to be the signal for the students to rise; and as he was unwilling to lose any opportunity of observing the customs of the place he got out of bed and dressed himself. He left his room at twenty minutes after six, and as he went downstairs heard the sound of footsteps in the *ambulacrum*—the large corridor where students and professors had been walking and talking before Benediction on the previous evening. No voice was audible, however; and when he reached the foot of the staircase he found some twenty or thirty of the theological students, or "divines" as they were called, walking to and

fro in perfect silence. He himself paced slowly
up and down, not speaking to any one, as it did
not seem customary, but wondering in his own
mind what could be the meaning of this silent
march. As the clock struck half-past six all
turned round with almost military precision and
went into church. Darlington followed them,
expecting to be pleased and interested by the
service, as he had been on the previous evening.
He was disappointed, however. All assembled in
their places, professors and students—excepting
the younger boys—but no service commenced.
Some had books open before them, which they
seemed to be reading; others were apparently
doing nothing, but remained kneeling perfectly
still, their faces buried in their hands. Darlington irreverently surmised that they had fallen
asleep.

Ten minutes of waiting for something to take
place was enough for his patience, and he arose
from the seat he had occupied in the ante-chapel,
and wandered through the adjoining corridors,
which led, as he found, to several smaller chapels,
which were sufficiently ornamented with carving
in wood and stone and with pictures of various

scriptural and historical subjects, to keep him occupied with their inspection until the sound of footsteps in the main chapel warned him, twenty minutes later, that some change was taking place in the monotonous proceedings therein. He hastened back, and found the younger boys all pouring in. Once in their places, they recited morning prayers, one of the divines reading the main portion, and all joining in the answers. Then came mass, a service familiar to Darlington in the course of his travels on the Continent. Each of the professors said his own mass in one of the chapels which Darlington had just been exploring. He followed Ashley, and listened to him for a time, and then quitted the church. He knew the mass, and did not care to see it through. He made his way to the Professors' parlour, where Dr. Russell, the President, and Ashley found him, reading a book, when they came in to breakfast. Darlington had been curious as to the meaning of the silence in church, and took the first opportunity of asking.

" It was the meditation," said Dr. Russell.

" I understand," replied Darlington, " a mystic contemplation and *reverie*, I suppose, such as

Comte was in the habit of indulging in every morning."

"No," said Dr. Russell, rather sharply; "it is not mystical, but very practical. It is a preparation for the duties of the day, and ends with a series of practical resolutions."

Darlington did not press Dr. Russell further, but took occasion, when the President was talking to some one else, to ask Ashley for a fuller explanation. Then he learnt that meditation had been customary in the Church from earliest times, that it had been systematised by St. Ignatius Loyola, that it consisted in reflection on a scene in our Lord's life, or on sin, or death, or any other important truth—an attempt to make it vivid in the mind, so as to have a real effect on conduct, including practical resolutions, and prayer for strength to carry them out. This was, he gathered, an ordinary type of meditation, though there were many technical modifications of it.

"You see," added Ashley to his explanation, "we believe that we are living in the midst of supernatural influences, and that our actions will affect, for good or ill, our fate for all eternity;

but these facts are easily forgotten *practically.* Meditation is intended to ensure what we speculatively believe having the effect on us which it ought to have. We think of these truths just as a father places before his spendthrift son the consequences of his folly and extravagance, which he already knows, but does not reflect on."

All this was very interesting to Darlington, and seemed to him logical and reasonable from Ashley's point of view. He then questioned him about the silence before they entered the chapel, and learnt that the students were supposed, in order to make sure of the thoughts in question taking root in their minds, to read the meditation the night before, and to think as little as possible of anything else until mass time next morning. To help them in this, strict silence was enjoined.

"From your account," Darlington said, "it seems to be a sort of retreat, such as I have known Catholics make abroad."

"Precisely," Ashley replied; "a miniature retreat."

He then explained that the tension on the

mind was so great that the younger boys were
not thought capable of it, but that at special
times they also had similar exercises allotted to
them—that is to say, during the regular formal
retreats which took place twice in the year.
Ashley watched with pleasure the interest which
Darlington showed in hearing the particulars of
the spiritual training of the students, and took
the earliest opportunity he could find to sound
him as to the effect of the previous night's conversation, now that he had had ten hours for
it to sink into his mind.

"Well," Ashley began, as he and Darlington
walked out of the breakfast-room together,
"have you thought over our last night's talk
at all? Are you ready to acquit us of being
unreasonable fanatics who believe, or profess
to believe, merely because religion suits our
taste?"

Darlington hesitated. "I thought," he said,
"that we had an interesting talk, and that there
was a good deal in what Walton said. I thought
that we got at the truth as far as we went, but I
can't see that he really proved his case against
me."

"Where did he fail then—what is your difficulty?" asked Ashley.

"I think," said Darlington, "that he analysed correctly the two sorts of wish with respect to a belief—one being the wish to manufacture or to nurse it as the case may be, the other the wish that it should be true. The one is readily father to the thought, the other makes one fear that what is wished for is too good to be true. One begets a belief like Bentley's theory of an imaginary editor of 'Paradise Lost,' the importance of which to him was not its truth, but its utility in affording him an hypothesis to rest upon which would warrant his continuing work which interested him. The other is the wish of Penelope for the return of Ulysses, which was so strong that she could not for a long time convince herself that it had come to pass. All this I see; and I think that in the sense which he explained the first class of belief has no great depth of root, while the other, from the caution and anxiety it implies, requires fully sufficient reasons and takes deep root."

"That is precisely what Walton was contending for," said Ashley.

"Wait a moment," Darlington continued. "Now for my point of divergence from him. He seemed to think it clear that the case of religious believers is of the latter type, whereas it seems to me that facts point to an opposite conclusion. Theirs is no case of breathless expectation of news—tidings of unspeakable happiness, which prevents them from daring to believe with confidence for fear of the shock of disappointment. On the contrary, the belief will not be verified for a long time to come, or at least a time which most people picture as indefinitely distant—the time of death. It is rather the continuance of habits and trains of thought endeared by constant association, just as Bentley wished to pursue the line of study which interested him; or in the case of converts, it is the attraction which religion has for them either by force of reaction, or from a natural interest in and taste for religious thoughts and ceremonies. There is no near prospect of a rough awakening from the dream, and so it is indulged."

"You certainly don't give us credit for much sincerity in our professions," said Ashley.

"You mistake me," replied Darlington; "I

don't for a moment think you are insincere. But I say that your principal motive—or one of your principal motives—for belief is a wish, hardly acknowledged perhaps in the case of those who have always believed, to cling to what is dear to you. This is not insincerity any more than a doctor is dishonest who has not probed far enough, and says there is no bullet in a wound when there really is. He thinks honestly that there is none. I am not sure that Bentley was insincere, though, of course, his is an extreme case. He did not care about the truth of his belief sufficiently to test its depth, to probe the bullet-wound thoroughly."

"I don't know that you would find it an easy matter to prove that to many of us religion would be so pleasant if we had not a really deep belief in its truth," said Ashley thoughtfully. "If you examined the details of the life of a Trappist monk (to take a strong case), I think you would find your account of the thing somewhat reversed. He does not believe in religion because he loves it, but he loves what is almost intolerable to flesh and blood because he has a deep belief that it is commanded by God. As to probing and testing the depth of his belief, it cannot surely be more effectually done than by his performance of a series of acts which are worse than worthless if his belief is not true. Surely that should suffice, if anything could, to make him attend seriously to the soundness and truth of his religion."

There was a pause of a few moments. Darlington was conscious that from the very nature of his attack it must be in constant danger of wounding the susceptibilities of a religious man; and the point he was now insisting upon was a peculiarly delicate one, as it seemed to border on a charge of insincerity. He had, therefore, two difficulties instead of one in replying. The first was to find a reply, and the second to express it without giving offence. Ashley, too, had an instinct that the conversation would run more freely if he could rid it of application to actual facts and charges against individuals; and, as his friend was silent, he resumed :—

"However, it is not of much use to appeal to the facts of the case. We have no measure which will positively ascertain the depth of belief in particular instances. Of course, you and I both judge according to our respective opportunities

for observation. I may perhaps claim to have
seen more of the details of the lives of religious
people, while you, no doubt, on your side will
charge me with being biassed and unfair. Walton's
argument, as I understood it, was rather an
assistance in judging how far and under what
circumstances one's wishes led one into fallacious
belief on the one hand and reasonable certainty
on the other, than a proof that no professing
Christians are led unreasonably by their wishes.
You brought a charge against us which implied
that religious enthusiasm was a sign that belief
was unreasonable, and that the wish to believe
leads to precipitancy in accepting dogmas; and
he showed on the other hand that neither of
these were unequivocal signs of fallacy,—that
enthusiasm need not be fanaticism, and that there
is a species of longing for belief which breeds
caution rather than precipitancy. He answered
the *primâ facie* objection which you made, and
which prevented your looking much further into
the question. He said, practically, this: ' Before
you dismiss religion as unreasonable because all
religious men have the wish to believe, make sure
what is the nature of the wish. True enough,

G

there is a wish that begets fallacious belief, but
there is another kind of wish which helps and
steadies the reason instead of impeding it. Be
sure, before you class all professors of religion
together as fanatics, that the eagerness they show
in the matter is of the former kind and not of the
latter.' And in answering so far your objection
he answered a doubt which might arise in his
own breast or in mine as to whether we may not
have been led astray by our wishes. The matter
must be always to a great extent one of personal
observation, and one cannot hope to record fully
or satisfactorily the results of one's observations.
Each individual must observe for himself. But
Walton's principle is a guide to us. It showed
that where we see reason to believe that much
depends or is staked on the *truth* of a belief, the
eagerness and zeal of a believer are far from being
signs that he has been hasty in believing, but rather
indicate a state of mind which would require a
deep and real assurance; and thus it enables us to
ascertain whether or no we have reason to fear that
the particular fallacy in question has ensnared
those with whom we are acquainted, and with still
greater certainty whether it has biassed our minds,

so far resolving religious belief in our own case into a part of moral probation where candour and conscientiousness are all-important."

They walked the length of the corridor in silence before Darlington resumed. "Look here," he said suddenly as if he had just found something, "here is your view of what you have been saying in a nut-shell. There is one kind of wish, you say, which makes a man prejudiced, another which makes him reasonable; one which leads him to dreamland, another which makes him confine himself strictly to realities. Now to keep my argument within reasonable limits, take the case of the evidences of Christianity—not to go back to still more fundamental questions. I find that among thinking men, all my acquaintance without exception who hold that they are, in the face of modern criticism, satisfactory and sufficient, are men who have a naturally religious bent of mind, a wish to believe. They are enthusiasts, and do not pretend to be impartial in the matter. Those who, being quite equally capable of understanding them, have no bias either way, say, at most, that they leave the question undecided. The only men who regard the matter

as settled on the affirmative side are, as I say,
men with religious cravings. Then I ask, which
kind of wish can I attribute to them? Can I
attribute the wish that makes one *cautious* and
slow when they are *less* cautious and *less* slow
in believing than those who are indifferent?" He
paused. "Can I?" he repeated.

Ashley looked puzzled. "I think," he said,
"that they may be on a different footing. Those
who are indifferent may take less pains in the
matter and dismiss it in comparative carelessness."

"No," persisted Darlington. "I speak of
people who have read all the standard books on
evidences, and who take really a great interest
in the whole matter—though, as I have said,
quite without any party feeling."

"It is so difficult," said Ashley, "to answer
a vague statement like yours. If I knew the
people to whom you refer, perhaps I should have
more to say in explanation;" and then he added
after a pause, "I remember that you quoted
yesterday the cases of Hume and Johnson. Well,
there I should say that there was at least as much
of the wish not to believe about Hume as of the
wish to believe in Johnson."

Ashley did not feel satisfied with the completeness of his own answer, and was somewhat
relieved at seeing Walton's portly form making
its way towards them.

"Good morning, Darlington," he said as he
approached. "I want you to walk over with me
to Greystone and see my mission and church.
You have found out already the difference between the new man and the old, and now I want
you to see something of his new mode of living,
and of the haunts and habits of the animal."

"I will go with pleasure," said Darlington.
"Would you believe it? we are already at this
early hour plunging into the very thick of theological argument, and you are just in time to
help us."

"Come then—and you come too, Ashley,"
said Walton. "We can talk as we walk."

Ashley excused himself. "I have a lecture to
give," he said; "but we shall meet again on
your return."

The other two started without more ado, and
Darlington lost no time in propounding his
theory to Walton in its new shape.

"How can I suppose that the wish of these

people is of the kind which makes belief slow
and difficult," he repeated, "when I find that
they believe sooner and more confidently than
those who have no wish in the matter? And
the only alternative I have left me—on your
own principles mark, Walton—is to suppose that
their wish is for the gratifications attendant on
belief, and not a deep desire—as you explained it
—for reasonable assurance of its truth."

"No doubt," said Walton musingly, "one who
is very anxious in the whole subject will see more
in the evidences than one who cares less about
the matter."

"That is the very thing I say," said Darlington. "He puts something into the evidence for
his pet doctrines which is not there. This is
plainly unreasonable. Evidence is evidence, and
must, if conclusive, convince any reasonable man.[1]
If I find that an impartial man is far from convinced, while one who is notoriously a partisan
professes himself satisfied, it is plain common
sense in me to ascribe it to prejudice."

---

[1] It may be as well to observe at the outset, for the benefit of
Catholic readers, that Walton's argument concerns exclusively
what theologians call the *judicium credibilitatis*, or act of the

"I don't know," replied Walton. "I think that is a very insufficient account of the matter. Impartiality is, true enough, a remedy for one intellectual vice. But there are others which may be quite as fatal. But first let us see what right you have to take it for granted that one who sees more in an argument than another does so through prejudice."

"Don't distort my statement," interrupted Darlington. "What I say is that where I find one estimate placed on arguments by all impartial critics, and another only by those who are notoriously and confessedly interested in one side of the question, it seems a plain conclusion that these last add the weight of their own bias where the arguments themselves are insufficient. If dispassionate thinkers of my acquaintance state clearly the arguments on both sides, can even, as Mr. Kegan Paul did in his recent paper,[1] show keen appreciation of the Christian and Catholic

intellect, whereby the evidences for revelation are judged to be convincing. He would, no doubt, consider any further question of technical theology out of place, as being unintelligible to one in Darlington's position.

[1] This conversation took place shortly after the appearance of Mr. Paul's essay entitled " Faith and Unfaith."

position, but finally declare the case 'not proven,' it seems plain to me that those who profess not only to see a probability but to possess absolute certainty on the believing side, being, as I have said, men of strong religious emotions, have been influenced by these emotions to believe what reason quite fails to establish. This is the plainest of conclusions, drawn on the principles of induction. It is an instance of one of Mill's canons. Here are phenomena agreeing in many respects, differing in two. On the one side there is the judicial temperament and suspense of judgement, or rather a decision that certainty is unattainable; on the other, strong religious cravings and a profession that certainty is attained. Reasoning power and evidence is the same in both cases, therefore the inevitable conclusion is that bias is at the root of this professed certainty."

Walton reflected a few moments before he spoke. He was trying to see at what point exactly the issue between them lay.

" It comes to this," he said at last. " If you have two men equally endowed with logical acuteness, the one without any bias, the other

anxious for religious belief, and if the former
considers, after reading the recognised works on
the subject, that the evidence is insufficient,
while the latter is convinced, you think it plain
that the latter is unreasonably biassed by his
wish—that those conditions which have determined his mind to belief as distinguished from
suspense of judgment, are not reasonable motives,
but prejudice."

"How can they be reasonable motives," said
Darlington, "when I am supposing that all the
reasons are equally known to the other? We
had better keep to our assumption of exactly
similar intellectual power, though of course there
is something rather grotesque in abstract principles
and typical cases."

"Now I should say," said Walton, slowly and
deliberately, "that granting every one of your
conditions, which as you say are of course never
accurately realized in fact, granting equal ability,
the same evidence before both, impartiality and
indifference on the one side, and great anxiety to
believe, if possible, on the other,—if the latter man
does believe, it is, as you say, owing—at least,
indirectly—to his craving and anxiety; but that

his belief is, or may very well be, eminently reasonable;" and he looked at Darlington, conscious that he was propounding what was at first sight a paradox.

"My dear Walton, how can a craving or wish which *hastens* belief do so reasonably? That is contrary to your own principles, and it is absurd. His wish can't put more into the evidence than there is in it."

"No," said Walton; "but it may make him *find* more than the other finds. I know what you are going to say," he said, as Darlington tried to interrupt him; "you are going to say that in our typical case the *same* evidence is before both. Granted. And they are both equally able to apprehend its logical force. Granted too. But the religious-minded man may get beyond its logical statement; he will *feel* its force"——

"Exactly," interrupted Darlington, "He will feel more than reason warrants. That is what I say. Such men let feeling do duty for reason."

"No," persisted Walton; "he does not substitute feeling; rather his feeling and his interest in the matter stir his reason to activity. There is a perception which one whose mind constantly dwells on a subject and who loves it acquires, which is beyond expression in words, and which is outside the sphere of verbal evidence; such a man acquires a special power in his estimate of evidence relating to the subject in question. Look at the musician who is devoted to a special composer. He can decide whether such a piece is or is not by him, merely by means of comparing it with the norm which his familiarity with the style of his favourite and his store of memories enable him to establish. He could not fully express the evidence on paper, but it is none the less evidence to him and *reasonably* apprehended, quite untinged with bias."

"That is not a fair comparison," rejoined Darlington; "a musical ear is a special gift. We are speaking of plain, straightforward evidence of historical facts. This appeals to that reasoning power which all mankind possess, and not to any special sense."

"The parallel is not exact," replied Walton, "but it will help me to explain what I mean. Let us take another typical case—this one shall be mine and not yours. To make my case more apposite, I suppose two men of equally good musical ear.

One has studied Mendelssohn carefully, the other far less so. A fragment of MS. music is found; there is considerable circumstantial evidence to show that it is by Mendelssohn. The man who is less closely acquainted with M_.ndelssohn's style, pronounces the case unproven; the other confidently asserts that it is not by Mendelssohn. The evidence is before both. Both are equally talented. One is devoted to Mendelssohn, the other has not made his works a special study. What is it which enables one to decide confidently and rightly while the other is in doubt? It is a certain personal perception acquired by the close attention which he has been led to give to the subject by his interest in Mendelssohn's works. One of the items of evidence on paper would be, 'There are passages which render it difficult to suppose that it is by Mendelssohn;' this is to be weighed against strong circumstantial evidence that it is by Mendelssohn. The MS. is in his handwriting, it is found among other fragments undoubtedly genuine. Now, though both critics hear the array of arguments, the particular one from internal evidence assumes gigantic proportions in the mind of one of them.

He manipulates it, so to speak, with a master's skill, gets out of it all that is to be got, and it decides the whole question. Why is this? Does not the other understand this particular item of evidence? Yes; but he has not acquired that personal power which enables him to *weigh it truly*—his appreciation of it is vague and (as he himself feels) uncertain. Thus though the evidence might be similarly *stated* by both—I mean that each might give a similar list of arguments *pro* and *con*—the relative weight attached by them to this particular item would differ *toto cælo*. One grasps the full force of what the other only half understands."

"Of course," said Darlington, rather impatiently. " All this is true enough of music. It is true of any art; and for this reason, that all that is really important in it is beyond the sphere of plain evidence and appeals to a special sense. If that sense has been cultivated in a particular direction, no doubt it is more acute in that direction."

"Yes, but mark," put in Walton, "the direct perception only affected a portion of the evidence."

"Oh! that was a mere trick of yours," said

Darlington. "You put this in for the sake of making the case seem at first sight parallel to religious evidence. It is plain that the real essence of your example is in the special musical perception of one man, which is not shared by the other. The rest of the evidence was mere pretence. You might as well suppose two men—one blind and the other not—judging of the evidence for the presence of a third party in a room. You might give a list of signs which both could perceive—a step heard unlike that of either, the sound of a cough unlike the accustomed cough of either—I won't say of a voice, as that would be unmistakable even by the blind man; the rustling of a newspaper proceeding apparently from a direction different from the position of either, and so forth. The blind man is not, you will say, certain; but the other clinches the argument by special personal perception, namely, the sight of his eyes. I think it would be shorter to say that one man sees a third party in the room, and the other hasn't eyes, so he can't see. Unless you take the Christian evidences out of the category of reasoning altogether, and suppose one man to have a sort of spiritual sense which the other has

not got, your parallel falls altogether. If you maintain, as you profess to, that they are a matter of
reasoning, just as a fact which has to be proved in
the law courts, this personal element of which you
speak finds no place at all. It is either another
term for a special sense, as in the case of art,
or it must mean prejudice. Fancy a juror who
refused to convict Lamson on the ground that
there was a personal element in his appreciation of the evidence which made him believe the
prisoner to be not guilty ! I think that if it were
afterwards discovered that he was a friend of
Lamson's, people would not be slow in suspecting what the nature of the personal element
was."

" Well, I will meet you on your own ground,"
said Walton, a little nettled at Darlington's confident tone, and at the apparent common sense of
his answer. " You have not treated my example
fairly, but I do not care to insist upon it at
present. I will take a case of ordinary circumstantial evidence. I maintain, in spite of all you
say, that there may be circumstances in which
one man may, from his knowledge of character or
from his acquaintance with particular persons, or

his intimate familiarity with the details of some science, take a different and a far truer view of evidence before a law court than the average educated juryman who has not this assistance. And his view may be purely personal in the sense that he is in possession of no further evidence on the subject; but facts in the existing evidence may be to him, on account of his antecedents, of different significance, and this will not indicate a prejudiced mind but rather special clearness of sight. Take for instance a charge of fraud against some one of whose integrity you are absolutely sure. My case will not be strong enough unless you think of some individual. There are many whom you *think* incapable of such a thing, but some whom you *know* to be so. I should imagine that one who knew Dr. Johnson or Dr. Arnold most intimately would have had the absolute assurance of which I speak in their regard."

"Oh! I quite agree," said Darlington, not thinking for the moment of the connection of his admission with the argument; "there are persons whose character is completely formed and fixed in uprightness, for whom a downright dishonourable act would be a moral impossibility. I could mention persons of whom I should say this from my own knowledge of them."

"Well then," resumed Walton, "suppose the strongest evidence of a circumstantial kind were brought against such a man, a juror, to whom this evidence is quite intelligible and convincing, would decide against him in spite of his previous good character. Your assurance that he is incapable of the act may have *some* weight, but little in comparison with the overwhelming evidence against him. You cannot convey to the juror the *personal knowledge* which is in your own mind, and the only indication you can give of it is to him vague and unreliable. He cannot be sure that you are not biassed, though you yourself may be conscious that you are not. He cannot distinguish the interested partisanship of a friend from the clear, serene feeling of certainty, begotten of intimate knowledge, which is in many cases its own guarantee that it corresponds with truth. Thus your own certainty of the man's innocence is, as I have said, personal and yet reasonable. Your judgment differs from that of the juror, though you have the same evidence

H

before you. The juror judges as nine-tenths of those who see the evidence would judge. But you, through your close acquaintance with the ground of one particular portion of the case for the defence—that portion which relates to the criminal's previous good character—have acquired a sense of its force which makes you able reasonably and confidently to differ from others in your estimate of the whole matter. And I would add a fact which seems to me important, that your judgment would carry with it a sense of *power* and *knowledge* as distinguished from a feeling of impotence to take another view, or inability to enter into it. The juryman would not have a feeling similar to yours. Your state of mind would be, 'I am perfectly sure;' his would be, 'the circumstances of the case are such and so significant that I see no room for doubt.'"

He looked at Darlington, but saw from his face that he was not following his remarks further, but was turning over the example in his mind.

"Well, Darlington," he continued, "will you allow some reason to a personal view of evidence in the case I have given?"

"You have yet to apply it to the real question

at issue," said Darlington; "and I cannot see where you will find in Paley or Butler anything at all parallel to the intimate knowledge we may have of a friend's character. But anyhow your instance seems to me unreal. Overwhelming evidence against a man of unblemished character is not a common thing, and practically the difference of view would be much less than you describe. The friend would be shocked at the evidence, and the juror would be slow to convict even on strong evidence if the prisoner were held by his friends to be a Dr. Arnold in integrity."

"Of course I stated an extreme case to point my moral," said Walton; "that I take to be the whole *rationale* of an illustration to show the working of a principle in an instance where it is unmistakable, in order that one may be ready to admit it in what is more complex and obscure. But I do not admit that my instance is unreal or improbable. The history of Lesurques and Dubosc was exactly a case in point. The story will be familiar to you from the English plays founded upon it. I remember Charles Kean in the *Courier of Lyons*, and you no doubt have seen Mr. Irving's last version of the same story in the

Lyons Mail. It was a case of mistaken identity, and took place in France in the last century. Lesurques was a man of good position and spotless integrity, and had been singularly fortunate and prosperous in his career. At least so he is represented in the play. He considers himself 'the happiest man that ever lived,' and the story of his death is consequently all the more tragic. The robbery of the Lyons mail took place at a posting-house kept by his father, and on the very night on which the crime was committed Lesurques himself was on the spot intent, as he said, on some act of kindness to his father. When the mail was robbed he was actually, it appeared, seen by several witnesses, among them his father, taking part in the crime and in the murders which accompanied it. The evidence against him was overwhelming, and on the strength of it he was guillotined; and too late it was discovered that the real criminal was a man called in the play Dubosc, resembling him exactly in features and general appearance.[1] Surely this is as strong a case as any imaginary one I could invent! The

---

[1] This discovery is in the play, previous to the time appointed for his execution; and he consequently escapes.

evidence was direct and apparently conclusive.
Mistaken identity was his only possible plea, and
he was quite unaware at the time of the existence
of this villain who was his exact counterpart;
and when challenged to prove an *alibi* was unable
to do so. His guilt seemed proved; and those
few friends who knew him and trusted him in
spite of all, must have appeared to the world at
large utterly beyond the reach of sensible argument. They were trusting to a vague, undefin-
able feeling, and going in the very teeth of evidence as conclusive as circumstantial evidence
could be; and yet if Lesurques were such a man
as I have supposed, and said to his friend, looking him full in the face, 'I declare before God
I am innocent,' the conviction produced, and
reasonably produced, in that friend would be
absolute and incapable of being shaken."

"Certainly that is a strong case," said Darlington; "but I should say that in reality the
friend and the outside world were not viewing
the *same* evidence. The friend had a past knowledge of Lesurques, which the jury and others
had not. Here was a separate item in the considerations before his mind."

"No doubt," replied Walton, "you may look at it so; but that does not affect what I say. Whether you call this personal element fresh evidence, or consider the evidence to be the verbal statement and the knowledge which colours it as imparting a perception to the mind in its estimate of it, it comes to the same. It is a mere question of words. What I want to show is that this element most frequently exists, and carries the mind to truth instead of prejudicing it."

"I think again," said Darlington, after a few minutes' reflection, "that knowledge of the character of a friend is very unique, and will hardly be found to help you if you are giving principles for the estimation of *historical* evidence. You can have no friendship with the dead, and a past fact is not proved by anything resembling personal acquaintance."

"Have patience," continued Walton. "I have given the case of knowledge of character first, because it seems to me to be a particularly strong instance of personal perceptions as affecting one's view of verbal evidence. It is not the only instance, though I believe that something very similar to it bears an important part in the

impression produced on each man by the study
of Christianity. What I wish to show is that in
all evidence there are items which appeal more or
less to personal perceptions, and that in many
cases those perceptions will differ in individuals,
without implying a want of candour in those
holding either view, but simply a lesser or greater
power of judging in the particular subject-
matter."

"Oh! you are going through all the cases
given in Newman's *Essay on Assent,* I suppose,"
said Darlington. "I quite allow that a good
general is a good judge of military position, a
good scholar of Tacitus' style, a man with a turn
for politics of a political situation, and the rest.
These are all questions of what is called 'implicit
reasoning.' I should have something to say on
this subject, but it is not the same as that of
which we now speak. I am purposely confining
myself to the recognised explicit arguments in
favour of Christ's divine mission and miraculous
history. Paley's *Evidences,* Liddon's *Bampton
Lectures,* Butler's *Analogy*—it is of such works
I speak. I am not supposing an intellect
which travels under ground, as it were, and

emerges, with no knowledge of the road it has
traversed, in a state of Christian belief—declaring
that, though it cannot give reasons for its conclusion, that is no sign that they do not exist,
but only that they are implicit. That is a special
puzzle which I am not at present trying to find
out. Let us keep to plain, explicit evidence.
There are many who profess that the recognised
explicit evidences suffice for them, and it is
enough for the present to consider them."

"What you say only helps to bring me to the
central point of my argument," said Walton.
"What I particularly want to show is that, even
where arguments are stated most explicitly, there
is a personal element in their full apprehension.
I can understand your considering the knowledge
of character of which I spoke as a conclusion
gained by implicit reason and *added* to the evidence. That is not the account I myself should
give, simply because the mind is so constantly
affected in its judgment by its store of impressions
formed by past experiences, that to isolate one
seems to me unscientific. However, let us now
take the plainest and most clearly stated evidence
we can think of. Some murderer has, as Lefroy

did, escaped from the police, and it is their business to trace him. He has been clearly traced to
Stoke-on-Trent. They find that a man answering to his description was seen at Stoke-on-Trent
station on the day after the murder a short time
before the 10.15 train started for London. Again
at Stone one of the porters noticed a similar man
in the same train in a first-class carriage; and
when the ticket-collector took the tickets at Wil-
lesden, he, too, noticed the man, who, it so happened, was unable for some time to find his ticket.
Further inquiry results in a similar declaration
on the part of five other porters. Now here is a
very simple chain of evidence. Any reasonable
mind on considering it would come to the conclusion that the man who was seen at Stoke had
in all probability gone to London. Here you will
say that there is no personal element in appreciating the evidence at all. Credible witnesses see
him at different places on the line, on close examination they give an exactly similar account of
his personal appearance and dress, and the conclusion is a mere matter of common sense. Now I
quite agree that all reasonable men will conclude
alike here; but I wish to point out that in each case

there is an exercise of personal judgment, though,
for reasons I shall give, the result is for each
the same.   There are certain suppositions which
would invalidate the conclusion.   The witnesses
may have committed perjury, in spite of the good
character they previously bore.   There may have
been a man exactly similar to the man seen at
Stoke, and dressed in the same way; and this
second man may have been the loser of his ticket,
while the original man may have been walking
on the platform to pass away his time, and left it
unperceived without entering the train.   Now,
as I have said, any reasonable man will dismiss
these suppositions — and why?   Is there any
clear logical statement which will disprove them?
Take one of them only—the first.   How can you
logically prove that eight men of unimpeachable
character have not every one of them committed
perjury (supposing that to be the only possible
flaw in the evidence), and that merely for the fun
of the thing and without any further motive?
You can't *prove* it, but it is wildly improbable.
And why do you judge it improbable?   Because
our knowledge of human nature tells us that men
do not do these things.   This is surely a decision

on personal grounds. No doubt these grounds are
shared by all men ; but they are personal to each.
The fact that all men have sufficient personal
experience of human nature to make their decision
in such a case the same, makes one forget, until
it is pointed out, that the decision is arrived at,
not by logical rule, but by a process similar to
that by which Lesurques' intimate friend was
convinced of his innocence, with this entirely
accidental difference—that in one case all have
the experience requisite for a true decision, in the
other case only a few."

"Oh! of course there is always judgment to
be exercised in weighing evidence," said Darlington. "Perhaps it would not have occurred to
me in the case you gave, as it is so simple that
one would hardly be at the pains to analyse it.
Just as one may never have reflected—any more
than M. Jourdain did, until it was pointed out
to him—that he had been talking prose all his life.
But I don't see what you gain by the long explanation you have just given. It seems to me much
ado about nothing. Because an exercise of
common sense is justified in the case you have
given, that is no proof that the view of an excited

enthusiast is warranted by reason. I should
rather say that your instance heightens the contrast I gave, and tells in my favour. It shows
that sober-minded men judge alike in matters of
evidence, and that their judgment is reliable."

" I am afraid that I shall have to be somewhat
tedious in my explanation," returned Walton,
" and shall only be able to draw out my meaning
by a dull train of examples, extorting admissions
out of you the full meaning of which you will not
see—in true Socratic style. But I will try to be
as brief as possible. The only point which I
insist upon in my example is what you have
granted : that even in the simplest evidence there
is an exercise of personal judgment amenable to
no law, but ratified by the mind's own positive
declaration."

" Clearly," said Darlington, rather impatiently,
" it is not all a logical train like Euclid."

"Now one step further," said Walton. " In
the example I have given the logical part of the
argument attracts most attention, because the
other part is plain, and is hardly expressed in
words. One would express the thing, " He was
seen at such a place and at such another place,

and therefore it is plain that he has gone to
London." One might even imagine a case where
this aspect would be more strongly exhibited."

"I see what you mean," said Darlington;
"you need not enlarge upon it."

"Let us now take a case," pursued Walton,
"where these proportions are reversed. To
avoid being more tedious than is absolutely
necessary I will plunge *in medias res* at once.
Let us take one of the very books you have
named — Liddon's *Bampton Lectures on the
Divinity of Christ.* Perhaps the third lecture
will suit our purpose as well as any. It is on
the work of our Lord in the world as a witness to
His divinity. He draws attention to the unique
history of the Jews, to the unpromising nature of
Christ's scheme, and its audacity; and yet the
calm confidence with which He proposes it, its
novelty, its realisation by powers and forces
unparalleled in the past history of the world, and
so forth. Now the mere logic of his argument is
of the simplest. It amounts to this: the phenomena of which I speak are such as to render
impossible the supposition that they are due to
anything short of special divine interposition;

therefore divine interposition must have taken place. The whole force of the argument lies in the judgment of the mind as to how far the antecedent proposition is warranted by the facts of the case."

"You speak truly, O Socrates!" said Darlington, laughing.

"That is to say," said Walton, waxing more earnest, " the just and right estimate of the argument depends principally, not on clearness of head, not on logical consecutiveness, but on the accurate gauging of on the one hand the marvellous facts of Jewish and Christian history, and on the other the powers and capabilities of unassisted human nature."

Darlington nodded assent.

" In other words, on this very personal element of which we have spoken. You read Liddon's lecture to a friend. You say at the end, ' Do you see Liddon's argument?' He replies at once, ' Oh yes! he states it most lucidly; I understand it thoroughly.' You press him: ' Do you think it powerful?' If he is a sensible man he replies, ' I will think it well over, and then I will tell you how it impresses me.' And it is this thinking it well over, this mental digestion, this personal apprehension of the considerations, which is the important and critical part of the matter."

Darlington did not say anything; but his face, when Walton looked at it, did not betoken agreement, but rather dissatisfaction at being unable at the moment to find words for his difference of opinion.

"Let us add to this argument in question," continued Walton, "that of Liddon's fourth lecture, in which he insists upon the unique personal character of Christ, on its moral beauty, its superhuman consistency, its possession of qualities incapable of co-existence in mere man, the lowliest humility together with the most absolute self-assertion, the contrast of His conscious greatness with the self-abasement of the prophets, His enthusiasm, and at the same time His 'sweet reasonableness' and entire freedom from fanaticism. Here is another argument calling, not for logical power, but for personal appreciation and just judgment."

Darlington had by this time shaped his difficulty. "You really are not touching my position in all you are saying," he insisted. "No doubt the particular arguments you are speaking of call rather for calm and true judgment than for a power of following a train of syllogisms. But, in the first place, they are only a tithe of the arguments available on the whole subject; and in the second place—even if we confine ourselves to them, as you are doing—my original objection holds good. It is plain that an unbiassed man will judge more truly than one who has strong religious emotions and a desire for belief. It is all very well for you to say that there is a personal element in the view that each man takes of the evidence. No doubt that is true in a sense; and it makes it impossible to put your finger on a fallacy as you can in mere logic. But the personal element, as you call it, is merely the exercise of the power of judging, which is far more likely to be correctly exercised by one who is perfectly unbiassed one way or the other, than by one whose reason is disturbed and prejudiced by a wish to come to one conclusion rather than another."

"Now we are really getting at what I want," said Walton. "I maintain that in estimating considerations such as I have mentioned, an active interest and sense of the importance of the conclusion to which they point, and a certain amount of emotional sympathy with them, are absolutely necessary. A man who does not apply his emotional and imaginative faculties cannot feel them, cannot get beyond the mere logic of them—that hard rind of truth (for it is true as far as it goes) which George Eliot lays down as the limit of the knowledge of the unimaginative and unsympathetic. The calm, lawyer-like man who studies the matter as though it were an illustration of some interesting legal principle, and not of deep practical importance to himself, stands no chance of knowing their full force. No doubt such a man runs no risk of overrating it, but he runs the greatest risk of underrating it."

"My dear Walton," interrupted Darlington, "what should we do if we accepted this strange theory of yours? We should have our law courts supplied by enthusiastic jurymen, or intimate friends of the prisoner or of the witnesses for the prosecution."

"No; the cases are not parallel," said Walton, a little puzzled. "The law courts go on the principle that it is better to acquit a guilty man than to hang one who is innocent. They dare

I

not risk the influence of bias either way. The outside world cannot be sure what is partisanship and what intimate knowledge. Personal certainty of which I speak is safeguarded, as we shall see, by a sense of personal responsibility. The certainty is your own, and if you conclude wrongly it affects yourself and no one else. The case is different with the juror, who is deciding what affects another, and fears no evil result to himself from a wrong decision. But we shall see this better later on. Let me first show more clearly what I mean in reference to the arguments from our Lord's work and personal character. It is a very different thing to know a fact and believe it on the one hand, and on the other realize fully its significance. This of course is taken for granted in our whole ascetical and spiritual system. The monk commences his day by an hour of meditation in order that that world of whose existence he has no doubt may be to him a reality as well as a truth. The sinner makes no question that hell exists; but if its existence were vividly before him—were, as I have termed it, realized by him—it would be so strong a motive as infallibly to deter him from sin. And the same principle holds good with regard not only to the effect of belief on our acts, but also to the weight of one belief as an argument for another. Cardinal Newman says in one of his sermons that it is a very easy thing for a man to sit in his study leading a student's life and to work out theological problems about hell without feeling the slightest difficulty in believing in its existence. But if he comes to mix with his kind, and it stands before him as a reality that hell must be at all events for some human beings, for A or B or C or D, he then finds it very hard to think it possible that even the worst of those with whom he has been in contact could be deserving of so awful a doom. Here is an instance of an argument so commonly urged *against* Catholic belief not being done justice to or felt in its full force because it is not realized. I don't of course believe the argument to be conclusive, but I give it as an instance which, so far, will tell for your view of one of our dogmas, and which at the same time illustrates the principle on which I am insisting. Now just as a man may apprehend the idea of eternal punishment, and may understand the difficulty raised against its justice from

the absence of all proportion between the sin of
a finite being and a penalty which shall have no
end, and yet may not feel the real force of the
objection because he realizes neither of the considerations which it involves, so may a man
apprehend the meaning of Liddon's argument
from Christ's unique personal character, and yet
quite fail to be duly affected by it. He may hold
with Mill that it is indubitably historical, and
with Rousseau that the invention of such a career
and personality is a more incredible hypothesis
than their existence. And yet he may wholly fail
to realize the argument to be derived from it
either for His divine mission or actual divinity."

" It is rather a vague argument," said Darlington; " I should be sorry to stake much on it. I
think that Mill's own conclusion with respect to
it—that Christ's life was a perfect translation of
the rule of right from the abstract to the concrete,
and that He had *possibly* some special mission to
mankind—is quite as much as you can hope to
draw from it."

" Its statement is vague, certainly," replied
Walton; " but I think it has far greater significance than you suppose to one who has studied

it reverently. But let us keep to the point. What I insist on is that the strength of the argument, such as it is, does not depend on the considerations involved in it being known, but on their being realized. I do not say that it is by itself conclusive. But it has considerable force, and that force is only perceived where Liddon's statements are felt as realities as well as believed in as truths. I want you to mark this contrast between knowing a fact and realizing it. Enoch Arden thought he could bear to see his wife after she had become another's, thinking him dead. But he had judged wrongly. Miriam had told him all, and he knew what he had to expect. But he had not fully realized it. It was as yet a sort of dream. When he saw the reality and felt vividly all that was involved in what had happened, he broke down. Do you remember the lines :—

> ' Now when the dead man, come to life, beheld
> His wife, his wife no more, and saw the babe
> Hers, yet not his, upon the father's knee,
> And all the warmth, the peace and happiness ' . . .

And so forth—

> ' Then he, *tho' Miriam Lane had told him all,*
> *Because things seen are mightier than things heard,*
> Staggered and shook, holding the branch, and feared
> To send abroad a shrill and terrible cry ! '

Grignon, in that amusing play of Scribe's, *La Bataille des Dames*, can face all dangers in imagination, but when they come in reality he is an arrant coward. And though the contrast between his attitude towards imaginary dangers and real ones is of course exaggerated for the sake of amusing the audience, it is sufficiently true to nature to illustrate what I say. In the pictures he forms the dangers are not, to him, realities, and he believes that he can face them. The spirit of his heroic mother possesses him, and he promises himself all possible soldierly achievement. But in the field of battle or in time of real danger the caution of his prudent father prevails, and it is only when he cannot fail to realize his danger that he gauges accurately his own powers. Here, then, is another aspect of the personal element in the estimate of arguments. The individual effort to transform a dead fact into a living reality is absolutely essential in such arguments. And if I am to be philosophical over it, I should describe it, in the case of historical facts, as consisting, at least partly, in the endeavour to clothe that which is apprehended in the first instance by the intellect only—involving of course some faint picture of

the imagination—with the emotion and imagination which it would naturally have excited in the
actual witnesses. Not as though one were to
take the feelings of an excited mob, and the exaggerated conclusions which they might draw in
their excitement, as infallible guides, but rather
endeavouring so vividly to picture historical
scenes and characters by means of those elements
of emotion and imagination which constitute the
actor's power of sympathy, that they, in turn,
affect us as they would have affected us had we
ourselves been among the mob."

"What you are speaking of," said Darlington,
"seems to resemble the gift of an historian like
Gibbon, who could make past facts stand out
with wonderful vividness. I don't know," he
added, smiling, "whether he will help you as an
instance of its religious effects."

Walton was pursuing his own line of thought,
and unconsciously suggested the answer to Darlington's question.

"I have just said," he continued, "that the
actor's power of sympathy constitutes an element
in what I have called realizing a scene or an historical character. But I think that there is some-

thing beyond this mere emotional aspect of it. There is a deep sense that it is a fact, with practical consequences and effects on the world around, and possibly on yourself."

" I don't quite see your meaning," said Darlington. " It seems to me that the emotional appreciation of which you spoke involves that, and that which you speak of now is nothing additional."

" No," pursued Walton; " I think that there is something over and above emotion—deeper than emotion. Grignon may have had the vividest possible emotional picture of his dangers in the battle-field, and was as brave as a lion; but when danger was actually present, and he steadily felt that it concerned him, and might lead to practical results of a serious nature in connection with his own comfort, his courage evaporated. I think it was Charles Kemble who used to relate how he felt Mrs. Siddons' tears streaming down over his own face when he played Arthur. Yet human grief which concerns facts has something far deeper than the actor's sympathy with it. Mrs. Siddons could have wept had she lost a child in the play; but the aching sense of reality, with all its consequences which the death of her own child would have aroused, could never have found place on the stage.   There is one side of belief which is closely allied with emotion and imagination ; another with facts, consequences, and action.   Bain, I think, had this latter element in his mind when he spoke of belief as being ' readiness to act.' "

Walton paused, feeling that he had not fully expressed his meaning, and yet not at the moment seeing his way further.

" I am afraid," he continued, " that I am rather fragmentary and scrappy.   But I think some of the most important psychological truths are hard to express quite clearly.   They are recondite in proportion to their depth and intimate connection with ourselves.   Newman says of certain motives for religious belief that we cannot see them, just as we cannot see ourselves, and in defence of my own imperfect account I can only cite George Eliot's expression.   Do you remember how she speaks somewhere of ' that complex, fragmentary, doubt-provoking knowledge which we call truth ? ' "

" I think I see your meaning, though, all the same," said Darlington, reflectively.

"Anyhow," continued Walton, "be the analysis what it may, this realizing facts as distinct from merely knowing them is a very important fact in giving just weight to many an argument. Do you remember, in the second act of Meyerbeer's *Etoile du Nord*, the scene in which Pietro, who has had too much to drink, condemns Caterina to be shot, not fully realizing who she is? I remember that Faure's rendering of the play of feeling and mind used to bring very vividly before me the contrast of which I speak. He made it evident that he had recognised her, long before he had sufficiently recovered his mental balance to realize (I can find no other word) the effects of what he had done and the necessity for immediate action. At length it comes upon him in full force. What had been a sort of dream, with no facts for consequences, and no necessity for personal effort, suddenly appears to him as it really is bound up with his own responsibility and with the very life of her who is dearest to him. He makes a tremendous effort, throws off the effects of the wine in a moment, and sends in an agony of mind to countermand the sentence —though he fears it may already be too late."

" I remember the scene well," said Darlington.
" Caterina is disguised as a soldier and strikes
Gritzenko, the corporal, when he reprimands her
for looking into Pietro's tent."

" Well, now," continued Walton, "let me try
and show more clearly, by an example, how this
element of realizing may affect the conclusions
one draws from a certain class of arguments.
Some one says in 1780: 'The awful misery and
oppression which the common people are under-
going in France, must lead before long to a
terrible revolution;' and he mentions fact after
fact. This is at the dinner-table of M. le Marquis de R——, who is entertaining guests at his
château. He is sipping his claret and listens with
much interest. Some days afterwards other
guests are dining with him, and he repeats with
great gusto, as giving a zest to the entertain-
ment, the sensational facts which he has heard.
' F—— thinks,' he adds, 'that it must ere long
lead to a general revolution.' Neither the facts
nor the revolution are realities to him. He
could not draw the conclusion, though he can
repeat it. He does not *see* it, because it is the
vivid apprehension of the facts which leads to it,

and that apprehension he has not got. But M. le Comte de V——, who is at his table, takes in every word with hungry avidity. After each of the details he is visibly shocked, and the whole company remark how moody he becomes. He leaves early. 'Do you know, M. le Marquis,' asks one of the guests, 'what makes our friend so much out of sorts?' M. le Marquis does not know. 'I think the facts you mentioned came home to him rather unpleasantly. He has been something of an absentee from his property, and his agent appears to have ill-treated his tenants past all bearing. They make little distinction between servant and chief, and one of them attempted to stab him the other day. I fancy that your account of the oppression which goes on, often unknown to the landlord, made him feel what reason there might be to apprehend another attempt of the same kind.' But in truth M. le Comte has been made very serious by the details in question. The facts which were forced on his attention in connection with the attempt on his own life, have given him a keen sense of the possibilities of serious results, and the whole question—both the oppression and the consequent danger to himself and to the State—is very real in his mind. You see at once my meaning—the danger was a conclusion from the reality of the facts. The Count realized the facts, and so could infer the danger. The Marquis could not see the reality of the danger, because excellent claret and the dinner-party were much more real to him than anything else."

"The Count might easily be carried too far by his fears," Darlington remarked.

"As usual," said Walton, laughing, "you always want me to answer everything at once. Hear me out first. All I say at present is that there was a *just* conclusion to be drawn, and no one could draw it by logic, but only by realizing the facts and their significance. I think, then," he continued after a pause, "that this element of realizing the considerations involved in some of the Christian evidences, throws considerable light on your original question. The man who is intensely in earnest and anxious for knowledge, if it is really attainable, will take far more pains than another to do this. If he is anxious in the way I described for a belief, if it is only know-

able as true, his anxiety tells both ways ; it guards
him, as we saw yesterday, against overestimating
the force of arguments, and yet at the same time
it stimulates him to use his utmost endeavour to
appreciate fully all that may help him to find or
hold what he is so anxious for. ' Where there's
a will there's a way,' says the proverb. A man
who is bent on passing an examination, finds his
faculties stimulated and works with a concen-
trated energy and success, which he cannot command in the absence of such an incitement.
And in the same way, if a man feels keenly that
religious belief, if attainable, is all-important to
him, his whole nature becomes intensified in the
search for it. He will marshal the evidences
which are offered to lead him to it with an
activity of mind, and will ponder them with an
earnestness, which one who views the whole
matter as an interesting problem only can never
possess ; and so he is convinced sooner, not
through bias, but because the arguments, instead
of remaining logical *formulæ* outside him, have
taken full possession of his soul, and are felt not
as vague ideas, but as facts vividly realized in all
their connection with each other and with him-

self. To draw, then, for the moment only, a
partial conclusion, is it not at least a possible
hypothesis, that when Gibbon gave five causes
which he thought would account for the spread
of Christianity by merely natural forces, he had
failed, through want of earnestness, both to
gauge correctly the powers of human nature,
and to realize the significance of the phenomena with which he dealt? And when Locke,
on the other hand, said that he found in Scripture alone, sufficient proof of the divinity of
Christianity, or, to take a more satisfactory instance, when Newman finds in the very phenomena which Gibbon explains away the strongest
confirmation of his belief, is it not, on the
principles we have allowed, at least possible
that he may have intensely realized and felt
the true force of what would have been but
partially understood by one who was less in
earnest?"

"Well," said Darlington, slowly, "one could
not prove that it had not been so."

"I don't know whether you see," continued
Walton, smiling, "that you have already considerably moved from your original position.

You commenced by saying that if one who was anxious for religious conviction was satisfied by evidence which, to one who was indifferent, seemed insufficient, it was plain that he had been biassed; and now you grant that it is at least possible that his anxiety may have made him see what the other failed to see."

Darlington did not answer at once. "I will hear you out," he said, after a few moments. "I have a good deal to say, but I want thoroughly to understand you first."

"There is another very important element in Christianity," Walton continued, "which depends in the last resort on personal effort for its due appreciation. We have already spoken of remarkable traits in the character of Christ, which should stand before the mind as real facts in order that their true significance may be felt. But I think it possible to get beyond the mere knowledge of admirable qualities. We have seen this in the case of a personal friend. There is sometimes a knowledge of him so intimate as to give a sort of electric sympathy with what goes on in his mind, and enable us to predict within certain limits what would be his action in this or that case—and still more confidently what it would *not* be. The process whereby this takes place is worth noting. It may be, and often is, in some such way as the following :—First we see him perform isolated acts of generosity, public spirit, tenderness of sympathy, and so forth. Gradually these instances are multiplied. We see by dint of constant association with him that they are no products of a changeable spirit, which may give an alms through physical pity one day and have a dependent turned out into the street to starve through ill-temper or dyspepsia the next. Thus in time the acts assume a harmony, and are regarded as qualities. Not only has he done this or that act of kindness or high-mindedness, but we see that he *is* kind and *is* high-minded. But we may know this of many a man—know very many of his good qualities and frailties too— without feeling, as we should express it, that we thoroughly understand him. There is an addi- tional blending into harmony which we do not yet perceive—and that is the proportion and in- terconnection of his various qualities which form his *character*. Once we know the forces at work in the motion of the heavenly bodies, we can cal-

K

culate the position of a planet which has not
been directly observed. The discovery of Neptune
was, as you know, made in this way. We have
the key both to phenomena we have observed and
to those we have not. We have found it by a
careful study of those we can observe. The character is the key to a man's qualities; and there
is a perception of *character*, as distinct from a
mere knowledge of various qualities, which close
and constant study will give, and which enables
us to predict, with greater or less certainty, what
a man would do under circumstances in which
we have not seen him. It cannot be exactly
expressed, but it consists in a feeling that, as I
have put it, we *understand* the man in question;
just as an actor must understand the character he
depicts, being unable, if he is intelligent, to represent a mere series of abstract virtues and vices.
Now surely a very close and constant study of
Scripture gives this sort of knowledge of Christ
—not perhaps quite in the same degree as actual
knowledge of a living man could do, but still in
a very remarkable degree. It is clear that the
subtle perception shown in Canon Liddon's
lecture of the significance of the juxtaposition in

Christ of certain qualities is, to a great extent,[1] the result of close familiarity with, and contemplation of, Christ's character in the Gospels; and I say that this same process may make one's perception keener and keener until at last His personality stands out clearly, and is seen in its full harmony. I do not pretend to draw out fully the results of this; but I have seen the fact strikingly illustrated in many holy men I know, whose minds dwell constantly on sacred history. The Christian spirit is a phrase commonly used, and really implies as its foundation much the same thing. When a man feels that his knowledge of our Lord is so intimate that he knows almost on each occasion what He would have done in similar circumstances, he acquires a trust in Him which renders it inconceivable that He should have professed to be what He was not in reality. And, again, he feels the unsatisfactory nature, the inconsistency and discord, of any view other than the Christian. M. Renan's Christ, with His "tenderness of a vague poetry" towards women, His mixture of belief in Himself with

---

[1] I say "to a great extent," because he may have been aided by the remarks of other commentators.

hypocrisy and the rest—which have to be explained as being Oriental, that is to say, outside the experience of ordinary readers—is to him an impossible personage. His subtle perception of the harmonious interconnection of qualities in the Scriptural Christ makes him feel that you cannot destroy as much as M. Renan does without destroying more. His reason revolts against the theory that the raising of Lazarus was a pious fraud quietly acquiesced in by Christ for the sake of gaining influence. The 'frightful accesses of enthusiasm' which Renan speaks of jar unspeakably with the calm and divine dignity which he has come to know and worship. He has a keen insight into the links between one quality and another, and draws, not from a broad half-stated argument, but by finest and subtlest perception, the old conclusion 'Christus si non Deus non bonus.' M. Renan is, he sees, a bad character-artist. He has the dull perceptions and want of taste of one who ornaments a Gothic church in the Italian style.[1] A real artist would destroy more, or destroy nothing."

[1] The hideous Renascence altar in Amiens Cathedral is an instance of the effect of such a combination.

"All this seems to me very hazy and unreli-able," said Darlington.

"No doubt," replied Walton; "the very re-mark which you would have made to the friend of Lesurques who was true to him, and believed him innocent in the face of the strongest evidence. He would have said, 'I know him too well to think him capable of this crime, or to believe that he could assure me of his innocence, being all the while guilty; such ideas are out of harmony with his whole character;' and you would have laughed at him for trusting this vague, unreliable impression rather than the strong, definite, tan-gible evidence on the other side. It is of the essence of this kind of personal experience that its record should appear to another unsatisfactory, vague;—that is the very strength of my argument. There is something beyond the verbal record, which that record cannot convey."

"But, after all," said Darlington, "Scripture *is* but the verbal record."

"Don't let us split straws," replied Walton. "You see plainly what I mean. Boswell's *John-son* gives to the careful student a knowledge of Johnson far more accurate than can be analysed verbally, and surely one is not paradoxical if one attributes the same power to the scriptural sketch of our Lord. The record in Scripture or in Boswell's Life is not an *analysis*, but a sketch which has to be carefully studied to be appreciated. Here, then, is another instance in which it is not the logical apprehension of the verbal statement, but the individual effort to penetrate behind the words, which enables one to understand the force of the argument in question ; and I would ask, Who is the man who is most likely to do such arguments ample justice ? I should say, to put it on the lowest ground, that in this, as in all else, the instinct of self-preservation holds good. If a man is (as religious-minded men are) filled with the thought that knowledge of the highest kind possible and greatest personal importance is offered to him, which if not attained, by his own fault, may result in the greatest unhappiness to himself, it is plain that he will do his best to attain to it, and devour all considerations placed before him as the necessary conditions with hungry avidity. And if at the same time he is conscious that his whole life must be based on that knowledge, if attained, he will be unable to stake his all on an uncertainty, and will be thus protected from any unduly sanguine view in the matter. In other words, the greater the effort he makes to realise the gravity of the whole issue and its practical bearing on himself, the more likely is he, as a consequence, to enter fully and justly into all that tends to throw light on what he feels to be so important."

"I see that he should be anxious for truth in the abstract," said Darlington ; " but it seems to me unjust and dangerous that he should be anxious to join the believing side any more than the Agnostic side in any discussion. Both parties stand in the same position with reference to an ordinary inquirer, and he should do equal justice to both—striving, as you say, to enter fully into and make real and vivid in his mind the considerations on the Christian side, but testing their validity by criticism, and not forgetting to study and do justice to the objections which the sceptic has to urge, or which arise in his own mind. One side has no greater claim on him than the other ; to give greater attention to one seems to me prejudiced and unphilosophical in attitude.

Both are candidates for approval on the same footing."

"No—thrice no!" said Walton; "they are *not* on the same footing. The Christian Church offers you not an alternative view of life but a prize, the greatest of prizes—certain knowledge about the highest interest of life. The Agnostic offers a blank—ignorance. Do your best to obtain the prize, and if indeed you find it to be unattainable, then, and not till then, rest contented with the blank."

Darlington looked puzzled, but said nothing.

"This then secures," Walton continued, "the reasonable attitude towards the credentials of Christ and His Church—anxiety to gain the knowledge they offer, and not a simple wish for abstract truth; or rather a keen desire to know the truth on that particular subject as distinguished from the rather apathetic and uninterested impartiality which seems to me involved in a mere vague wish for truth in the abstract. It is plain that the more effort you make to see the truth of Christianity, the more evident it will become, if you fail to do so, that it is incapable of being proved; so that whichever view is the true one, the greater the effort the surer the knowledge. Then, again, the anxiety and interest must be, as we have seen, for this knowledge as felt to concern ourselves practically, and not for a problem interesting as intellectual food only. 'Seek, and ye shall find.' This has a wide application even intellectually. If you seek for interesting arguments you will find them, and in them is your reward. And if you seek to know that which affects your highest interests, you will find that, too, if it is to be found. If you feel it all-important that revelation, if divine, should be known to you as such, your efforts to enter into and understand its credentials will be all the more intense and successful. 'La vérité,' says Lacordaire, 'est une œuvre de silence et de la reflexion.' You will ponder deeply the considerations pointing to its divine origin. They will be to you realities; subtle and significant connections in them will unfold themselves in the course of your reverent meditation, which would escape one who studied them with a different aim and spirit."

"I must study all sides of the question," said Darlington ; "that is only common sense."

"Master one thing at a time," replied Walton.

" If you are constantly touching on every point
of view you will be Jack of all trades—or views
—and masters of none.   Study that which professes to be the one solution of the awful enigma
of existence, make sure that you have felt deeply
and truly its harmony and the significance of its
proofs, conscious that true personal appreciation
differs widely from the external view which the
average mind takes at first sight.   At least do
not wash out one picture and replace it by another
until you are sure that you have done all in your
power to appreciate the first."

Darlington persisted, " You must study the
other side."

" I will talk that out some other time," said
Walton ; " it would lead us too far now.   If our
arguments are convincing, that is no more necessary in such a case than it is to hear all the
sophistical objections which might be made to
one of Euclid's conclusions.   At present all I contend for is that you should *first* give yourself every
chance of appreciating the true significance of
Christian evidence, and for this purpose you must,
at least for the time, concentrate your endeavours."

"Anyhow," Darlington said, "these principles of yours apply only to a very narrow portion of Christian evidences. Christ's character, the growth of the Church, and destruction of Jerusalem are of course remarkable facts, but they are only a tithe of the evidences. There is the whole question as to the alleged miracles—most of all, the Resurrection. Then, again, a critical inquiry is necessary as to how far we are justified in believing many of the marvellous facts alleged. Much of the Scripture is disputed as to its authenticity. These and kindred matters call for dry historical research in which all your personal effort, and reflection, and realising, and the rest have no place. They only affect a small portion of the argument."

"I think their effect is far wider than you suppose," said Walton. "I cannot pretend in a moment to show how wide, but I may suggest one or two ways in which they act. No doubt their province is in the first place what we have been considering. But look at their indirect influence. Consider, for one thing, the practical effect upon a mind which is engaged, even over the purely critical portion of the argument, of a

keen sense of the uniqueness of the history and
character of Christ and His Church. One who
goes to work without this feels, now-a-days, that
he is defending a losing cause when he attempts
to state the Christian side. All the presumption
against a breach of nature's uniformity. His
own constant experience has worked deep into
his mind a sense of the improbability of what is
unlike the general course of phenomena. Then,
again, he is cowed by the ridicule of a host of
scientific writers who laugh at his superstition
and lack of 'exact thought.' Surely he is in
danger of under-estimating the arguments, as
feeling it highly improbable, before he looks at
them, that they can be conclusive. Whereas, if
he has truly realised that Christ's character is—to
use the language of one whose whole education
and belief were opposed to Christianity—unlike
that of all other men, whether predecessors or
successors, that the story of the Jewish people
and of the Christian Church is quite unparalleled
in history, and so forth, then, even apart from
the actual and direct proof to be found in these
considerations, he has in his mind that which
will give him heart and hope in his study of what

remains. His mind, instead of being filled, as most minds are, and biassed by a sense of the improbability of what is unfamiliar, is impregnated with the thought of a great marvel. If one marvel is true, why should not other marvels follow in its train? Then, again, the probabilities of the case are affected at every turn. The realizing of what Christians have done gives an idea of human nature and its powers quite different from that which naturally and habitually exists in the average lounger of this civilised age. And as we have seen, our estimate of human powers and qualities affects constantly the weight which we attach to circumstantial evidence. It affects the *à priori* probabilities of the case, and may give an entirely different view of the credibility of witnesses. If we realize the conduct of the Apostles after the Resurrection, we see how deep must have been their assurance of its truth. Such an hypothesis as a pious fraud in the matter becomes at once absurd. If you reflect you will see that a similar effect is produced upon the weight of evidence at every turn. I do not say that those considerations which depend *entirely* on the personal effort and qualities I have mentioned for their just appreciation—the internal evidences of credibility as Catholic theologians call them—are in themselves conclusive; but I do say, and I can at least speak for my own case, that a mind may be perplexed and depressed by the intricacy and subtlety of critical questions, and that considerations similar to those of which I speak, if vividly present to the mind, may, by their own direct weight combined with the indirect assistance and courage they give in appreciating more complicated arguments, raise such a mind to a clear and serene sense of certainty in the whole matter, not necessarily solving every difficulty, but giving ample assurance that it has found the truth."

" Yes ; it is all a *feeling,* and an *assurance,* and the like," said Darlington. " I cannot trust such things; they are too vague."

" Vague to you," returned Walton, " as the criteria of good art to one who is no artist, or—I say it again—the account which Lesarques' friend would give of his intimate knowledge of him to one who had not that knowledge. It is the account that is vague; the perception itself you can't judge of because you haven't got it. How often am I to say this?"

But Darlington was growing tired, and hardly listened. "No sensible man," he insisted, "could trust to such uncertain shadows. He might have an impression that he saw further than another, but no real confidence."

"Well; there, at least, plain facts are against you," said Walton. "It would be absurd in me to attempt to enumerate a tithe of the great thinkers who have based their whole lives on a view of religious evidence which was so far personal and outside its logic as to differ from the view which they themselves originally took. Lacordaire's conversion is as good an instance as can be given of a change of this kind. I think it is in one of his 'letters to young men' that he says that when he looks back and tries to find the logical causes of his conversion, he can see nothing beyond the Christian evidences, which had always been familiar to him, but which had failed to *impress themselves on him* as long as he was surrounded by the atmosphere of sceptical discussion which he breathed in at the University; but which convinced him after quiet, earnest reflection. In other words, while his interest in them was purely speculative, they were insufficient; but when he meditated reverently upon them, not confusing his mind with every theory and objection under the sun, but allowing these particular considerations to assert themselves and sink deep into him, he realized their importance and significance, and felt their conclusiveness. His appreciation of them became more complete, and raised his mind from scepticism to a clear vision of the truth."

Darlington shook his head and looked incredulous.

"Well," said Walton, "I don't want to insist further upon the degree of confidence which may be reasonable, as that is going beyond my original point, and raises many other questions. I should say, even apart from any supernatural element, that there is much more in the mind than we have contemplated to account for its certainty in such a matter. All that I here maintain is a view exactly opposite to the one you enunciated as a sort of truism at starting. You said that of two men equally able to understand the logic of a series of arguments in favour

of the divine origin of Christ's mission and revelation, the cool-headed and impartial man is
plainly he who will judge them at their true
worth rather than the religious-minded man. I
think I have gone far towards showing that, on
the contrary, the logical apprehension being an
extremely minor point, the mind which passively
receives their logic with impartial indifference is
the worst possible judge of their true worth ; and
perhaps all the more so for this reason, that he
is so completely satisfied with his ready grasp
and neat presentment of the verbal shell, that he
never dreams that the whole strength of the
argument lies beyond it."

"You will find it hard to reverse my ideas so
much," said Darlington, "as to make me believe
that impartiality is not essential to a correct
estimate of all evidence. Other things may be
needed as well, but that most of all."

Walton looked annoyed. "You either cannot
or will not see my meaning," he said. "Of course
no one denies that partiality in the sense of bias
is to be avoided. What I have been pointing
out is that indifference is fatal, and earnestness
for knowledge essential. What would you say

L

if Newton professed himself indifferent as to whether he succeeded in making fresh astronomical discoveries, or failed? Should you say that that showed the needful attitude of impartiality which ensured the evidence being valued correctly, and that without it he would run the risk of rash conclusions, and would believe on an insufficient induction? or should you not rather say that if he cared so little about it he would probably not succeed if discovery were at all difficult? I say again that we must secure ourselves from being biassed by our wishes, not as the juryman does, by indifference as to results, but as the physical explorer does, by a longing for true knowledge."

This seemed to strike Darlington. "True," he said, "that is a new aspect of what you insisted on last night. It brings before me better than anything you have said in connection with our present subject."

"There is Greystone," said Walton, pointing to a small church two or three hundred yards in front, with a house adjoining it; "let me try and sum up what I have said before we reach it. I have endeavoured to point out how different the

value of a certain class of arguments may appear
according as our personal appreciation of them is
complete or incomplete; and that this difference
is not such as can be expressed in the statement
of them, but must be felt by the individual mind,
because their force does not lie in the logic of
them, but in the reality, significance, and connection of the facts they bind together. We
have seen that familiarity with a subject, acquaintance with a personality, the effort to realise truths
in all their bearing, are therefore of such assistance
to our apprehension that they may show an argument to be very strong and definite which would
without their assistance appear very weak and
vague. This may account for the fact that
persons deeply interested in the truth of a
particular allegation find arguments in its favour
conclusive which to others are not so, without
any supposition of bias or prejudice. Then again,
so far as the true personal estimate of arguments
implies effort and pains taken, it is more likely
to be attained to by him who is anxious to be
certain of the truth these arguments profess to
establish, as feeling it of the greatest practical
importance to himself to have correct knowledge

on the subject, than by him whose interest in the
matter is speculative and purely intellectual—the
instinct of self-preservation being, as I have said,
the strongest of stimulants in such a case. And
a similar instinct is, as I explained yesterday,
our best safeguard against being hurried pre-
maturely into belief by bias. Then we saw that
a considerable portion of the Christian evidences
are of such a nature as to depend for their force
almost entirely upon the personal appreciation of
the individual, and so to come under the principles
I have mentioned; and that these evidences play,
indirectly, a very important part in the whole
argument. This being so, I have said that the
attitude which you supposed to be truly philosophical is, in their regard, unphilosophical. A
state of mind which implies equal readiness to be
satisfied with Christian belief on the one side and
Agnosticism on the other affords no guarantee
that the necessary effort will be made to realise
and appreciate the force of the considerations
whereby the truth of Christianity is established.
An active speculative interest in all views is no
sign that the patient reflection and reverent consideration which are necessary if the Christian

arguments are really to touch us, will be given.
Indifference as to results shows that there is no
sense of the danger of ignorance and the blessedness of knowledge. And the mind which fails to
realize such truths as these may well fail to realize
much more. Absence of passion suggests apathy.
A judicial frame of mind will not seem the most
hopeful to one who remembers that ' the kingdom
of heaven suffereth violence, and the violent carry
it away.' No doubt these qualities are admirable
in a court of law for the very same reason that
they are out of place here. The very fact that
twelve jurymen are to agree upon their verdict
implies that the evidence is to be of such a kind
as to *exclude* special personal appreciation, such as
knowledge of an individual character. The outside world cannot be sure whether such professed
knowledge is in a particular case genuine or the
result of bias, therefore it is eliminated. Then
again, so far as personal effort is required, one
may say that its necessity is to some extent pre-
cluded by the work of counsel. The facts of the
case and their connection and significance are
depicted by them in glowing terms, so that all
that is required on the part of the jurymen is to

be receptive and impartial. In religious inquiry, on the contrary, the really philosophical and reasonable frame of mind is one involving earnestness, effort, and sense of the gravity of the issues, and of the blessedness of knowledge. A passion for knowledge is as indispensable to the religious as to the scientific inquirer. And if knowledge be attained, who can doubt that what is so beautiful will beget enthusiasm —nay, that an enthusiastic love for its beauty will help in the perception of its truth—just as a love for the goodness of my father may make me delight more and more in his society, and so become more intimately acquainted with his character?"

They had reached Greystone and entered the wicker gate of the presbytery garden. "You have not proved to me," Darlington said, "that religious believers fulfil the necessary conditions even if I grant what you have been saying."

"No," replied Walton, "and I do not suppose it is certain that all who profess belief do. Of course the same faults which prevent others from feeling the force of the evidences would, naturally speaking, prevent them too. And it is quite impossible to judge with certainty how far those faults do or do not exist in others, although with regard to ourselves we can be more certain; in the same way as a master cannot know with cer-tainty whether a boy's assertion that he has found his lesson too difficult is genuine or a mere pre-text for idleness; though the boy will know in his heart of hearts whether his efforts have been honest and ungrudging. I think, though, that I have shown certain qualities to be *essential* to a right estimate of the question, which qualities are associated with one's idea of an earnest and reli-gious mind. I do not wish to sit in judgment on professing believers. I only show that the reli-gious bent of mind which you spoke of as making you suspect bias and unfairness may well indicate the presence, not of unreasonable partisanship, but of a sense of the reality of religious problems which lights up with reality all that bears on them—just as our friend the Count, who felt the reality of his danger, saw the significance of each reason for fresh apprehension—of the blessedness of knowledge, of the wretchedness of ignorance, of the wickedness of apathy in such a matter, of possible personal danger in culpable ignorance, and consequently a passion for knowledge. And this sort of wish to believe, so born and so bred, this longing for certain knowledge concerning the highest and noblest interests of life, may well be not only no obstacle, but an indispensable assistance to what is in the highest sense a reasonable view of the matter."

"You seem to me to place the whole thing now on a footing which makes it impossible for many to value your creed correctly," said Darlington. "What am I to do if my mind is not religious but sceptical?"

"I don't want you to drive me to personalities," returned Walton; "but of course the question goes further back. One must ask how far a man may not be responsible for the fact that he is not awake to a real danger, or has lost the highest instincts of his nature by neglect."

"Well, it is useless arguing the matter on this footing," said Darlington. "If I have lost my eyes, arguing won't make me see."

"No," said Walton, "but if you give a fallacious simile, I will answer you by one nearer the mark. One who has not skated for thirty years may not at once be able to keep on his legs, but after he has been on the ice half an hour, trying hard, the old habit returns. Anyhow," he added, "to put it on the lowest grounds of common sense, that passion for religious knowledge which arises from a sense of possible personal danger and responsibility seems to me the only reasonable attitude for one who is awake and in use of his senses. We won't discuss this further now," he said, as Darlington attempted to speak, "or we shall never see anything of the church or presbytery. I merely end by saying that you may have my full mind, that for one who professes ignorance, and hears many able men, whose mode of life is based on the belief they profess, declare that knowledge is capable of being attained by one who is thoroughly in earnest, and that if by one's own fault it is not attained, the most terrible punishment will ensue, the reasonable attitude must involve such a sense of possible personal danger as will beget a desire for more knowledge. Then again, the apathy of a Hume or a Gibbon on the bed of death is from any point of view *unreasonable*—even more so, if possible, for an Agnostic than for a believer, as he has no clear knowledge of a merciful Providence, which is a

certain guarantee of just treatment. A sense of
the insecurity of ignorance, and the consequent
longing for knowledge, is as much the only
reasonable attitude in such a man as in one who
is told seriously by some, who profess to have
good reasons for knowing, that there are dangerous precipices here and there among the hills
where he is rambling on a pitch-dark night."

"I reserve my defence," said Darlington, as
they entered the presbytery grounds; "we shall,
as you say, do no justice to your architecture and
vestments if we go on talking." But he could not
help adding: "To me, though, it seems that stirring
oneself up to a frenzy of fear about things outside our ken, which we cannot control, is folly. I
do not constantly think of railway accidents when
I am in a train, because it would do me no good.
Fear is meant as a protection, and should not be
indulged in where it is of no practical use."

"And that is where we join issue," said
Walton. "I say that it *is* a protection in religious inquiry, and that it *does* lead to knowledge
and the consequent aversion of danger. You
have never tried the experiment, and I have,
experto crede."

And they walked into the house without another word, and were greeted by Walton's housekeeper, who asked if she should have luncheon ready for them after they had seen the church.

Greystone Church was a very simply constructed Gothic edifice of stone, and its chief interest to Darlington lay in the fact that it was the scene of the work to which Walton was devoting his life and energies. The house adjoining it was meagrely furnished, and Walton's study seemed little better fitted up than a monk's cell. The only article in it which attracted attention was a large wooden crucifix with a beautiful ivory figure, carved, evidently, with the greatest care and skill. This stood on the table at which Walton was accustomed to sit.

"It is very handsome," assented Walton to his friend's comment on it; and, in answer to his further questions as to the reason for placing it in front of his desk, he explained : " It is a very common custom with us. Out of sight, out of mind, you know. It helps one to keep the true object of life before one. It is another recognition of the principle we have been talking of— the necessity of keeping constantly before the mind the thoughts on which belief rests, that they may support both our faith and our hope."

In the church Darlington observed the "Stations of the Cross," and Walton gave him the information he required with respect to them also. "They are, as you see," he said, "pictures representing the different scenes of the Passion. The people walk in procession every Friday, stopping at each while I read an account of the scene it represents, and praying for strength and forgiveness at every station before going on to the next. It makes them think: it makes them realize all that our Lord has done for them. 'With desolation is all the world made desolate, because no man thinketh in his heart.'"

They walked back to Sandown in comparative silence. Darlington could not help having a certain feeling of moral inferiority after he had heard some of the details of Walton's self-denying life. "Still," he argued to himself, "such a feeling is quite unreasonable. Walton's self-denial and devotion are based upon a belief which to me is unreal and superstitious. No doubt, if I were called upon to work for a great cause which really appealed to me, I should not

be found wanting. All I lack is opportunity and
motive." Possibly, however, even after he had
said this to himself, he had a lingering doubt as
to whether he were not partly responsible for his
lack of opportunity. But such a frame of mind
was unusual with him and unpleasant, and he
cast it off before they reached home. No attempt
was made by either to resume serious conversation. Both felt that they had had quite enough
of it, and neither saw much chance of producing
any marked impression on the other. Darlington's frame of mind was one with which Walton
was well acquainted. The latter had been sub-
jected to the very same influences at Muriel in
years gone by, and had worked his way through
every argument and consideration by which his
friend was still influenced. The apparent absence
of any impression produced upon Darlington
during the conversation set Walton thinking.
How was it that two minds so similar to each
other in their very choice of arguments should
come to such opposite conclusions? And then
he remembered that there had been a time when
scepticism had enjoyed a short reign in his own
mind. He had thought out and faced the very

considerations which he had endeavoured—he was conscious with what imperfect success—to place before his friend, and he had been for some time unconvinced by them. An event had then happened,—a misfortune, which had for a time embittered his life and thrown him back in great seriousness upon religion, and the very same train of thought which in his previous state of active and irresponsible speculation he had dismissed as an insufficient basis for belief, broke upon him with a new force and cogency when he was thus brought face to face with the realities of life. And, remembering this, he moralised and came once more to the very conclusion which he had endeavoured to impress upon Darlington, that it is a very different thing to state a fact and to realize it; to express an argument and to feel its force; and that it is only a recognition on the part of the Church of a very plain and obvious law of the human reason which induces her to recommend a system of spiritual training which gives the reasons for belief every chance of "biting," if I may use the term—of being felt in their full weight and significance, as well as heard and known as facts.

THE great Orme's Head at Llandudno, with the charming sea breezes and sea views it offers to those who walk round it on a bright spring day, was the theatre of another discussion between Walton and Darlington on the wish for religious belief. A year and a half had gone by since Darlington had visited Sandown, and their meeting at the same hotel at Llandudno was purely accidental. Walton was to leave the place on the afternoon following the day of Darlington's arrival, and anxious—partly from a feeling of duty and partly from the interest he took in Darlington's character and history—to have some conversation with him as to his present frame of mind on matters of religion, he proposed a walk, *tête-à-tête*, for the following morning. Not that Walton was in a general way over-ready for such discussions, or anxious to force them on others; but he thought that he had discerned something in Darlington's mind, when they had met at Sandown, which led him to hope that real good might be done in its measure by talking to him. There was in him real candour and a complete absence of that tendency to object for the sake of objecting or argue for the sake of arguing, which is a sure and plain sign that discussion will come to no good. Walton felt that if two men were on the whole looking for the same thing—truth, they might at all events approach nearer to understanding one another, and that this circumstance which he thought he had perceived at Sandown with reference to Darlington and himself, removed their discussions widely from such things as they are generally carried on between men of opposite convictions, who are occupied for the most part, as a rule, in finding and elaborating arguments, each in favour of his own foregone conclusion, rather than in weighing conscientiously what is urged on both sides, modifying their own statements where they are seen, in the light of others, to be exaggerated, and adopting what seems true, irrespective of its apparent conflict with their own views.

A bright April morning promised to give the

great Orme every chance of offering them his very best of breezes and scenes; but long before they had reached him light conversation had given place to serious, and the beautiful blue water of the Llandudno bay appealed to them in vain for admiration, and passed unnoticed and without effect on them, absorbed as they were in their discussion, except, perhaps, that it may have helped to stimulate their minds, and conspired with the sea breezes and cloudless sky in giving freshness and interest to a subject which might else have grown tedious now and again.

" I suppose," Walton said, " that you have forgotten all about our ' wish to believe ' conversations at Sandown when you came down there last year with Ashley ? "

" No, indeed, I haven't," said Darlington; " they set me thinking a good deal. I have often gone over the whole question in my own mind since I left you."

" Well, and with what result ? "

Darlington smiled and did not answer at once. " I'm afraid," he said, " if you talked to me now you would find me a more confirmed sceptic than ever."

M

Walton made no reply, as he saw that Darlington was preparing to explain himself further.

"I must say," the latter went on, "that I thought the whole line you took was a very ingenious mixture of truth and falsehood. You stated clearly and cleverly certain truths which one must assent to, and then by a sort of logical sleight-of-hand you juggled in a falsehood to suit your book, and presented the argument anew, falsehood and all, as though I had accepted it without reserve. In our first talk you contended, rightly, that great anxiety to find something of great importance to be true tends to make one slow of belief,—that the man who has a couple of thousand on the boat-race does not lightly believe he has won; and then, when this much was established, you assumed that it was equally agreed that a religious enthusiast had this sort of caution-breeding wish. When we walked to Greystone, again, you went through a long list of examples to show that a thirst for true knowledge might quicken the mind in acquiring it, and then proceeded to talk as though the 'wish to believe' and the 'thirst for knowledge' were convertible terms."

"Come," interrupted Walton, "you will hardly question that in these days the very title you accept—Agnostic—is a confession that this is so. You can hardly deny that if religious knowledge is attainable it must take the form of religious belief. The wish, then, for definite belief is the same, on religious matters, as the wish for knowledge."

"No," said Darlington, in a tone indicating a somewhat contradictory vein, "I don't admit that at all. Socrates said of old, that in this one respect was he wiser than other men, that they, whereas they knew nothing, thought they knew something, he, on the contrary, was conscious that he knew nothing. If one is ignorant, the highest knowledge is to be aware of one's ignorance."

Walton was too much taken aback by this view to say anything at the moment, but Darlington soon went on—

"I quite demur to your assumption that your belief is a high state to aim at. Nothing that is false can be high, and it gives you an unfair advantage in your argument—or rather in the rhetoric of your argument—to assume that positive religious belief is a thing which an exalted mind must necessarily aim at, as constituting the only *knowledge* conceivable on the subject. The knowledge of the limit of one's own faculties is the really high knowledge. Suppose a man comes to me and says he dreamed last night he saw the man in the moon. He saw him vividly, and is convinced that he exists. He had had a strong cup of green tea before going to bed, and in consequence had had many visions, and among them that. He asks me to try green tea to-night, and to see if it won't lead to my seeing the man in the moon. I tell him I don't care to try the experiment, and he reproaches me with my want of earnestness in the matter. 'The only knowledge offered,' he says, 'on that subject is a belief in the man in the moon. Are you mean-minded enough to rest content with blank ignorance? You should wish to believe, for the wish to believe is clearly here the wish for knowledge.' I reply that on such a subject the highest knowledge is a knowledge of the limits of my reasoning and knowing power; that I am sure no such vision of the man in the moon can be real evidence of his existence; that the impressions of a dream are not trustworthy means to knowledge, and so I quite deny that the wish to believe is a wish for knowledge."

"Now I aver," said Walton, "that it is you who are juggling and slipping into your parallel something completely unlike the circumstances of the case we are dealing with. You allowed at all events in our last talk that there *is* much more to be got out of religious argument by one who has a keen sense of the personal importance of the matter to himself, than by one who views it without this stimulus to his mind. You have no right to parallel specially keen insight in reasoning to what one sees in a dream."

"Oh! of course," said Darlington, "that is overstated by me. But I do think that in essence it holds good. I think that the attempt to extract certain knowledge out of the stock religious arguments is almost as wild as the profession that a nightmare tells you the truth."

"You have never had the stimulus of an earnest wish to believe," said Walton, "and so you cannot tell what it will do in the matter. Until you have given your mind to the whole question with the dispositions I have spoken to you of, you can have no right to pronounce certainty unattainable. You can only say that you have not attained to it."

"I have the impartial wish for truth," said Darlington. "I consider that this is all the *stimulus* which you really showed as being necessary—nay, not apathetic," he continued, reading Walton's objection in his eye, "impartial in the highest sense, a keenness that truth may prevail, in whatever direction it may lie. You can want no more than this. Such a wish makes one feel the necessity of doing one's best in the matter, and of doing ample justice to the whole case."

"It does not give the power," Walton said. "A man can't labour without hoping for success. If the process of religious conviction in one who is in search of truth involves, as we have seen, sustained personal effort, the impartial hope that truth may prevail will not light up his mind in its journey along the path pointed out as leading to belief. If the path be rugged, as the path of hopeless effort must be, he will abandon it. He must have the hope that the considerations he is pondering will lead to something, and that is, in

the sense I have explained, the wish to believe if
it be possible to do so reasonably. The belief held
out is at least and at lowest parallel to the glimpse
of a possible new discovery which the astronomer
may get, and you will scarcely maintain that he
is prompted in following it up by a mere *abstract*
love of truth. He trusts that this *particular*
thing will prove true. Suppose there are signs of
the existence of a hitherto undiscovered planet.
He at once follows up the clue, not with a mere
wish to know the truth in the abstract, but with
a very strong wish to find more clues, and ultimately to find convincing reasons for believing
that the planet exists. His love of truth is
directed to a hope for discovery in this particular
matter. This it is which stimulates his efforts.
And this is, as I say, the wish to believe if reasonable belief is possible—a wish for conviction that
what seems probable is true. The only reason
why the wish to believe has ever been opposed to
the wish for truth is because it is so frequently
an insincere wish—a wish to maintain or hold a
thing, and not the wish to know it to be true—
that we are unaccustomed to think of it in this
latter aspect. It is in reality the concrete form

which the abstract wish for truth constantly
takes."

But this seemed too strange a conclusion for
Darlington to accept it. "You cannot," he said,
"identify things so different. According to you,
the partisan is a philosopher."

Walton reflected as to how he could convey his
meaning better.

"I amend my phrase," he soon said. "I will
not call the wish to believe the wish for truth,
but, as I did at first, the wish for knowledge.
Not but that these two may be explained as being
the same, but because I think it will show where
your fallacy lies. The wish for truth is often
taken to mean merely the wish to avoid error in
reasoning—the wish not to draw any conclusion
beyond what is warranted by one's premises. In
this sense an indifferent man who merely states
that he does not know whether the soul is im-
mortal or not, or whether natural or revealed
religion be true or not, may have a wish for truth
which cannot be identified with a wish to believe.
But it is at the point where some one comes to
him and says, 'If you bestir yourself there is
more to be known,' that he has to show whether

he has this merely negative wish for truth or in addition the positive wish for all attainable truth, the wish for knowledge. And it is only this last wish that in all active investigation of the different lines in which knowledge is proposed must take the form of the wish to believe."

Darlington, however, could not get rid of the feeling that this was all paradoxical, and ran counter to received expressions and acknowledged axioms.

"Let me try," Walton continued, "to put what I am saying in a fresh light. The wish to believe which I have advocated is, as you will remember, intimately bound up with the sense of the importance to oneself, often to one's own safety, of true knowledge on the subject in question. This it is which raises it to a passion, and it is on its being a passion that its effect in intensifying one's whole nature depends. Now one cannot have a passion for an abstraction. The wish for knowledge in the abstract, if very intense, must fix itself, must direct itself, must spend its energy in some definite work. It casts about it for some concrete means of satisfaction. A man struggling in the water in fear of drowning has a wish for abstract safety. But this expresses itself in his adoption of the most promising means of attaining to safety. He catches hold of some floating wood, tries to construct a raft, lashing it together by means of ropes he has found. Here we see his wish for safety in the abstract converting itself into the hope that he may succeed in these definite endeavours to find safety. Similarly, the man wishing for abstract religious knowledge casts about him for a clue. In what direction is he to seek it? Mark, again, it is *knowledge* he wants, and not merely truth negatively, which is content with indolent ignorance, under the plea that such a state includes no false convictions, as including no convictions at all on the subject-matter. I say then he casts about for a clue, and when he sees something which appeals to him as being possibly the knowledge he seeks, his wish for truth—or as I prefer to call it, for *knowledge—becomes* the wish to believe. Here is what he has been looking for. Here is the definite direction in which he is to look for truth. I am looking for the will of John Jones of Birmingham at Somerset House, as I have reason to believe that it contains information which is of some importance to me. I only know within twenty years the date of his death, and there are many John Joneses. Each one I find I hope to be John Jones of Birmingham. I look at his will carefully. My wish for the abstract true John Jones of Birmingham becomes a wish that this concrete John Jones may be the one I want. And I reason thus. If this be indeed the true John Jones, I have found what I wanted and my labour is over; and so that is my first wish. And then there is this additional consideration; if he be not the true John Jones, I have at all events, by doing my best to ascertain whether he *be* the true John Jones, clearly proved that he is *not*, and so have narrowed the channel of my search. I check him off in my note-book as a false John Jones, and so when I come again to search I shall know at all events that the will bearing the date in question is not the one I want, and so shall have one will the less to look through. Again, if I find other things besides the name which lead me to suspect that it may be the right Jones, I pay my shilling and read the will through, having an additional motive for

so doing. Though he *may* not be the John Jones
I want, these may be signs that he is a relation
—a father or an uncle—and some of the information I require may be in this will. And so, I say,
the man who is looking for religious truth takes
what is promising and beautiful. Can this be
the knowledge I am seeking for? he asks. It is
so noble, so elevating, so consoling, so practically
helpful to him, that he trusts it may. His wish
for religious truth becomes the wish to believe—
the hope that this may prove to be the truth,—
and at the same time he feels that the only way
to find truth is courageously to attempt to find it
in every direction which promises well. His first
hope is, then, that it may prove true—the wish
to believe, if belief be reasonable; his second
thought is 'anyhow let me do my best to see
whether or not it be true;' and he reflects at the
same time that it is highly improbable that what
commends itself so much to his own highest
instincts and to the moral nature of very many,
has not at least some admixture of truth in it;
and the keen search which the beautiful prospect
stimulates him to make will at all events have
this good result, that he will with quick eye note

and appropriate whatever grains of new knowledge there may be mixed up with superstition
and inaccurate theory."

Both walked on for some little time without
any further remark. Darlington was the first to
break the silence. "Suppose," he said, "that a
frightful religion presented itself—an immoral
religion with immoral deities—revengeful, unjust,
untruthful—a worse edition of the impure paganism of classical Greece. Would you advocate a
' wish to believe ' in it as the best way of investigating it? Should you say that the abstract wish
for knowledge as to what exists behind the veil
and what we are to look for after death must
take the shape of a wish to believe in such a
theory if it were propounded ? "

Walton reflected. "Wait a moment," he said.
" Let us see how far this would be really, and not
verbally only, the legitimate issue of what I have
been saying. I have said that the longing for
true knowledge as to our ultimate destiny, and as
to the invisible powers controlling the universe,
as to the import of the voice of conscience and of
our moral nature, as to the meaning of life, and
as to the end to be achieved, takes the shape,

when a promising clue is found, of a wish that it may prove a clue to real knowledge—a wish to believe. But, remember, the knowledge we seek and hope for is a knowledge *satisfying* our moral nature, and giving a definite meaning to those very aspirations which make us long for knowledge. We want an object of reverence which shall be real, and which shall at the same time explain and satisfy those instincts; an aim which can be definitely seen, towards which we may direct the moral action of our lives. But a wish to discover that impure and immoral deities are all that exist behind the veil, that there is no sanction to morality, and no basis in the aim and meaning of life for the moral impulses, would be the very opposite of this. It would be more like a wish to disbelieve. It would amount to a wish to disbelieve in anything great or noble, and a resigning of all hope for religious knowledge properly so called."

"And yet," said Darlington, "if knowledge is your one object, it seems to me that you should wish to know the best or the worst, whichever may be true."

"Yes," said Walton, "I grant it. But I

should *hope to find the best true.* And I contend still that your supposition would not be knowledge in the sense of ampler knowledge. Suppose it to be true, I should not blink its truth; but it would be by the keen sense of its horror and the intense wish to find it false that I should learn its truth."

" You must change your principles then," Darlington insisted. " If the wish for knowledge is supposed to make a man jump at every fresh theory that is started, and turn into a wish to believe in it, you have no right to make an exception where the particular knowledge proposed is different from that which you were prepared for."

" I must explain my principles more fully, not change them," said Walton. " You are giving me an opportunity of defining their limits and full nature for myself and for you. In the first place, you will remember that one of my conditions was that there should be a promising clue to knowledge—a clue sufficient to stimulate the mind with a hope for success. Now I should deny that any religion not satisfying in some degree our moral aspirations, *could* offer itself as a promising clue to knowledge. The very ground on which we believe that knowledge is attainable on the subject is that those aspirations point upwards to something above us. A religion, then, destitute of claim on our reverence has not even that condition of promising well which is essential to our being physically able to hope that it may turn out to be knowable as true. It is from the union of the internal evidence of the spiritual nature with the external credentials of the religion in question alone that certain knowledge is to be looked for, and a so-called religion which is not only unsupported but directly contradicted by the former, has in it no promising element. The highest ground it can assume is that of a possible truth, one of many possible truths, on the hypothesis that no truth in the matter is knowable by us. It is only the glimmer from above detected by conscience which can light up the soul with hope and give the wish to believe. Look at it again in this light. Compare the matter, as we have done, with strictly physical discovery. Suppose, *per impossibile*, that a theory were suddenly proposed which purported to show that the great laws governing the movements of the heavenly bodies on the Copernican hypothesis—

laws giving harmony and form and meaning to
observed facts—have been rashly generalised, and
do not square with fresh observations ; that in
reality the planets move at random and without
any one fixed law for all, and that the fixed law
had been assumed from some curious twist in our
observing faculties, which had given an apparent
regularity to their motions, just as one who
looked at objects through a succession of glasses
of various colour might rashly infer, if he did not
observe the glasses, that the objects in question
in passing along the road acquired these various
hues in regular sequence. Now I say that the
passion for knowledge in such a case as this
would not assume the shape of a wish to believe.
If this were true, there would be no *gain* of
knowledge, no fresh unity in our conception
of things, no further reduction of the chaos of
facts to the order of principles, but, on the contrary, the destruction of much that had been supposed to be knowledge. Thus to assume that
each fresh hypothesis must be examined, if the
principles I have advocated be correct, with a
wish to believe in *it*, is not to carry out but to
contradict those principles. There will be in

N

such a case a wish to believe, but to believe what
is *highest*, not what is lowest ; in good news, and
not in bad ; in what, if true, is ampler knowledge,
and not what, if true, is evidence that what had
been fondly reckoned ample knowledge is in
reality a delusion. And on exactly the same
principles a religion proposed which gives as a
full explanation of the basis of life, of creation,
of the aim to be lived for, of the ruling powers
over the universe, an account which, if true, would
show that those very phenomena which we had
looked upon as clues to knowledge, as facts pointing to a great system, seen, it is true, imperfectly,
but which we had hoped to see more and more
plainly, indications of a law unifying creation,
and giving a meaning to our moral nature and to
life as a whole, giving a coherence to human
knowledge and an aim for human action, are a
delusion ; that what we had thought to be a light
from heaven is but an *ignis fatuus*, that

'He is only a cloud and a smoke who was once a pillar of fire,
The guess of a worm in the dust and the shadow of its desire;'

such an account, I say, when looked at by one
who has the passion for religious knowledge,
arouses at once a wish, not to believe it true,

but to believe it false. I conclude, then, by saying that it is no exception to my principles, but only their legitimate outcome, to say that the wish to believe, which I have explained as the reasonable and indispensable stimulus and assistance in the discovery of truths in the matter, is the wish to believe in something nobler, giving wider knowledge, giving also a knowledge which completes the half-arguments which had suggested our search, which elevates us in the sphere of being, and not knowledge which would show that all our aspirations were meaningless, and which is only a knowledge of the hopeless darkness which is our lot. And I have, I think, said enough on former occasions to show that if indeed the terrible hypothesis that there is no elevating knowledge to be gained were true, the wish to believe it untrue, if this wish be the offspring of the passion for true knowledge in what is all-important, would not blind us to the fact, but, on the contrary, would give a keen and painful sensitiveness to the misery of our fate."

Darlington, without exactly dissenting, felt still puzzled. The religion of immoral divinities seemed to him still to be knowledge proposed,

he said,—unpleasant tidings undoubtedly, but
still, if true, it must be knowledge. It proposed
to give an account of what was really existing
behind the veil. This must be proposing fresh
knowledge. No doubt if this involved exposing
the falsehood of what had formerly been reckoned
knowledge, it did not give fresh unity to our con-
ceptions; but a fresh truth, which involved the
overthrow of the most cherished idols, seemed to
be still in a real sense fresh knowledge. Walton
thought for a moment, and said—·

"That is merely an ambiguity in the word
knowledge. I expose it thus. The passion to
know all truth, which is the radical passion, in
what concerns one intimately, pleads 'let me know
the best or the worst, which ever is true; the best
being knowledge enlarging and ennobling, the
worst the fact (if so be) that such knowledge is
unattainable.' Thus the passion for enlarging
and ennobling knowledge is the first hope implied in the radical wish for all truth. It is a
wish that the truth may prove to be what is
best. And this last passion becomes, as we
have seen, a wish to believe in a definite theory
which promises well and offers a clue to the

enlarging and ennobling knowledge which is
longed for."

They walked on again in silence. And if the
reader observes that Darlington made no reply,
and that Walton was again the first to speak,
and is tempted to exclaim, "Dialogue indeed! it
would be better called monologue, Walton is
prosing all the time," I would ask him to bear in
mind a few facts in human nature as bearing
upon persons with the mental history of Darlington and Walton, and upon the stage which the
discussion had reached. Walton had, as we have
seen, passed through a mental phase very similar
to Darlington's, and consequently his thought
was, whether for good or for ill, ahead of Darlington's. Not, indeed, that he had further
materials for religious knowledge, but in so far
as he had digested, sorted, and arranged much
that was somewhat chaotic in his friend's mind,
a process which, whether rightly or wrongly per-
formed, whether leading to the lawful repose of
certainty or to the fool's paradise of prejudice,
was necessary before his mind could rest in a
decision of any kind. Darlington's silent and
listening attitude came then from the feeling that

he was having a good deal of useful mental work done for him, and that much that had been vague in his own mind was being arranged and classified, —a process which could not fail to help him to clear his thoughts, whether or no the arrangement was such as ultimately to satisfy him. His silence meant then that he felt he was learning, though not, as the too sanguine controversialist would hope, that he was accepting the ultimate conclusions towards which Walton's principles professed to converge. Again his difficulties lay less in the fact that he saw flaws in his friend's reasoning, but more in the novelty and paradox of much that he said ; and such difficulties do not suggest a mode of answering back or joining in the discussion, but rather a feeling of wonder and a wish for further explanation, until the paradox seems so intolerable as to prompt exclamation rather than argument, and appears to the listener to refute itself by its very strangeness. And as this point had not yet arrived Darlington remained silent, half listening and half musing. Walton, after a minute or so of silence, continued—

" I believe, though, that we have been speaking

of an impossible state of things. The moral instincts of humanity do not allow of the existence of an utterly immoral religion. All religions have contained a germ of truth—an element of true knowledge; and I still say that where there is an element of fresh knowledge in a religion, satisfying the cravings of our moral nature, where such a religion is on the whole a step upwards from our present state; if it be proposed as a whole the wish to believe is the reasonable attitude, though if it be the honest and conscientious wish I have spoken of, it will gradually cast off the superstitious beliefs, the ritual absurdities, and impure ceremonies which accompanied some forms of paganism, and will prepare the mind for fuller and more complete knowledge. This is undoubtedly the principle on which St. Paul went when he made use of the religion of the Corinthians, mixed up though it was with superstition, to lead them to the truth. Their religion had in it a ray of light from heaven, though refracted so often and through such varied *media* of prejudice, immoral habit, false legends, and corrupt teaching, that the direction whence it came was scarcely discernible. St. Paul's work was to point out the refracting *media,* to show that they dimmed the light and deceived them as to its true direction; and by teaching them and making them understand more clearly the laws of the light, to lead them to distinguish between the colour and appearance of it as it reached them and what it was in itself. And when they had learnt to do this, and longed to see the light with the naked eye in its true brightness coming straight from the throne of God, once they recognised and admitted that there were *media* which dimmed and perverted it, he gave them power to remove the *media;* and the light flooded their hearts and took possession of them. And they recognised that this true light which enlighteneth every man who cometh into the world was, when seen aright, the word of God which is taught in the Christian Gospel."

Darlington found his mind filled by this time with a new set of ideas, which did not readily take their place side by side with the principles which habitually dwelt there. There seemed to be an element of truth in all that Walton had been saying, and he was far too candid not to admit and to feel this. But on the other hand, it

seemed at variance with much which he had been
accustomed to regard as axiomatic. That one
interested in coming to one conclusion rather
than another should, under any circumstances, be
a better judge and view the state of the case more
truly than one with no prepossession, seemed to
contradict canons of reasoning so generally acknowledged that they must be substantially
sound and correct. Then again, that an enthusiastic man should have in any sense a quicker eye
for the truth than one whose reason worked in
the normal way, undisturbed by passion, was a
conception which took the edge off the familiar
contrast between the visionary and the man of
common sense, the fanatic and the sober-minded
man. And although Walton had, both on the
present occasion and in former conversations,
gone some way towards explaining the limits of
his theory, and that it differed from received
expressions rather than received opinions, that it
contradicted an exaggeration of a recognised
truth and not the truth itself, still these explan-
ations had not become sufficiently fixed in Darlington's mind to dispel the feeling of mistrust and
repugnance which this view of things aroused in

him. The qualifications which Walton had been introducing into his explanation were too minute and subtle to stay clearly in his mind on their first introduction; and much in the same way as a beautiful landscape seen but once dwells in the memory rather in its broad outlines, and in the emotional effect it wrought at first sight, than in all the qualifying details which give to it its true character and its full interest in the eye of an artist, so it was the broad aspect of Walton's theory which was uppermost in Darlington's mind, and the effect which had been produced on him at first hearing this strange canonisation of prejudice, emotion, and fanaticism, and the still stranger disparagement (as it seemed) of reasoning as it is carried on by a clever and impartial man. " Where is all this to end?" he thought to himself. " We may have enthusiasts for Catholicism, enthusiasts for Protestantism, enthusiasts for atheism. Each will claim to be right, and will appeal to his own enthusiasm as a witness to the truth of his creed. The only way in which we have been accustomed to look for a common measure of minds, and a truth which reasonable men shall recognise, has been by the elimination

of these elements of excitement and passion, by
the calming of the disturbed mind, and the
appeal to reason stripped of passion. Here is a
theory which is not content with tolerating
passion, but encourages it." He had not, as I
have said, got full hold of the root principle
which Walton was advocating, and which alone
could explain and limit properly his half-expressed
conclusions. He had not mastered the fact that
it was passionate reasoning and not passionate
feeling, an enthusiasm for ampler and higher
knowledge, the essence of whose beauty is its
truth, and not for a beautiful idea as such, which
Walton advocated, and that a very deep sense of
the all-importance of truth and the fatal con-
quences of error or ignorance may enable one
to gain assistance from the weapons of passion
and enthusiasm without any danger of their mis-
leading. He did not fully see that a weight
which is sure to overbalance the reason if not
counterbalanced by another weight, might make
it steadier and firmer if so counterbalanced.
Impassioned reasoning, guided by what Newman
calls the heart and the eye for truth, leads to
truth. But an equal amount of passion, without

the sense of responsibility and of the importance
of truth, carries the mind to any prejudice which
it is set on defending, much as wine may enliven
and render more intelligent the discourse of a
serious man, while it gets the better of another
and stops his speech altogether.   These elements
in Walton's theory he had understood, but had
not digested or assimilated.   How could they be a
sufficient explanation of the matter, he reasoned,
viewing the matter externally and without following them closely or endeavouring to see their full
bearing, when a contrary set of ideas are em-
bodied in the received first principles for judging
of all evidence?   This was the form in which
he put his difficulties when he next spoke to
Walton.

" How can you account," he said, " for the fact
that impartiality is always looked upon so much
as a first essential in the estimate of evidence that
once it is admitted that a man is not impartial
but interested especially in one side, enough has
been said, and it is assumed without further
argument that he is not a fair judge, that he will
lean to the side he favours?   This is an admitted
first principle in weighing historical evidence

as much as any other, and the proofs of Christianity *are*, of course, mainly historical. There must be a great truth at the root of so acknowledged an axiom; and even though I did not entirely see my way through the very different view you seem to take, I should be slow to abandon an intellectual rudder which has been reckoned serviceable and fitted for its work by all men in all ages."

"No doubt," said Walton, "there is a great truth at the root of it, and, properly explained and limited, I should never dream of denying it. Let us consider the matter a little closely. It will really be only the application of the very principles on which I have been insisting, and which you suppose to clash with it."

He paused, as though trying to get the issues clearly defined in his own mind.

"You ask me," he went on, "what right I have to advocate one set of principles for the true estimate of historical evidence, and another for judging of religious evidence; and again how it comes about, if my principles are the true ones for religious inquiry, that so different a set of principles have passed into the very grammar of rules for weighing evidence. I think I can best answer your whole difficulty by showing why and in what class of cases the current principles are sound, and by pointing out how different individual religious inquiry is from such cases."

And he seemed again uncertain how to begin, and how to express his meaning at fullest advantage.

"I would first ask you to bear two things in mind," he said. "Firstly, to take the Christian evidences alone. A man who looks at them for purposes of religious inquiry must necessarily feel their strength to be supplemented by those very considerations in his own mind which prompted the inquiry. The need he has for a religion, the completeness of the satisfaction which Christianity affords to that need, the powerful appeal of Christ's character to his moral nature, here are specimens of the supplementary personal evidences which an individual inquirer has over and above the historical evidences viewed on their own merits. The *testimonium animæ naturaliter Christianæ*, however unscientific it may be as a proof, is now, as it ever has been, a very strong motive in the individual mind for belief. And the same remark applies to the testimony of the conscience to the truth of natural religion. I remember developing some of this more in full to you some time ago. The second thing I would have you bear in mind is that the evidences and proofs of natural and revealed religion, as looked at by the individual inquirer, are proofs of a matter on which knowledge is all-important to him, and on which the truth, whatever it may be, is fraught with momentous consequences in respect of his own destiny and bearing on his own immediate conduct."

"Yes, but that does not alter the character of the proofs," Darlington said. "The evidence in a case of a disputed will is fraught with great consequences to the plaintiff, and slight to the judge; but yet the proofs are there, not more or less visible to one than to the other, and must be judged by both according to the recognised rules."

"It does not alter the character of the proof," said Walton slowly. "No, but it changes the principles I should instil into each as essential to his judgment as to its true value being sound. Let me try and show my meaning. Just outside the town of Basingstoke there are the ruins

of an ancient chapel—the chapel of the Holy
Ghost, which was for many years the chapel
of the guild of the Holy Ghost—a teaching guild
of early origin. The chapel stands in the middle
of a very old burial ground, and antiquaries have
ascertained that there are good reasons for supposing that there were graves there as early as the
reign of King John. A theory has been started,
resting upon a certain amount of circumstantial
evidence, that while England was under an interdict in John's reign this place was first used as a
burial ground, burial in consecrated ground being
denied by the Church's ban. I do not care to go
very closely into the exact amount of evidence
which there is for this theory. There is the *à
priori* ground that it was not unfrequently the
custom in time of interdict to bury the dead
outside the city walls, and to consecrate the
ground as soon as the interdict was removed.
We will suppose that there is some additional
evidence. Now the antiquary who judges of
the evidence asks, we may suppose, what is his
most reasonable frame of mind—how can he
best secure himself, in judging of the evidence,
against a wrong conclusion. He is told that

he should look at the evidence with absolute
freedom from bias of any kind; that he should
have no wish to come to one conclusion rather
than another, but should be equally ready to see
the insufficiency or the sufficiency of the evidence.
This is no doubt sound advice. But on what
ground is it given? what are the reasons which
would make a wish to come to one particular
conclusion a dangerous element perverting his
judgment? Be it observed that the fact is gone
by both in itself and in its effects. The fact of
his decision being true or false, neither has nor
will have any effect on him. His interest in the
matter is purely speculative, although doubtless
lively enough. The facts concerning him practically and most vividly before his mind are the
present ruin and the associations which his re-
searches enable him to weave around it and the
stock of his discoveries which he is constantly
adding to. If he can decide that this account is
true, here is an additional element of interest
added to it, a fresh link in the chain of his discoveries, an additional completeness given to his
history of the place. The danger, then, against
which he is to guard is that of drawing a conclu-

sion, insufficiently proved as true but never provable as untrue, for the sake of the harmony and completeness it gives to his work. The intellectual error feared is not his wishing that one conclusion rather than another should be known as true, but that it should be accepted and adopted without sufficient reference to its truth. There is no element in the discovery of a matter the truth in which has no effect on the inquirer, which can ensure the interest in one side remaining identical with the interest in the *truth* of one side. Consequently the warning to be given is 'lean to neither side,' simply because in such a case leaning would imply a readiness to conclude without deep conviction. But take a case—a strong case—of a matter intimately affecting one's own personal safety, and you will find, I think, that the same principles do not apply. Documentary and verbal evidence is brought before the Czar of Russia tending to prove a plot for his assassination on the morrow ; on the other hand, some one comes to him, in whose opinion he has much confidence, and says he can prove that the evidence is a scare. Would any one say to the Czar that in looking at the whole case he was to have no interest in finding one side true rather than the other? Surely not. If one conclusion means personal danger, and the other safety, it would be of little use to give him such advice."

"Of little use, perhaps," said Darlington, "because he could not follow it. But it might nevertheless be the best advice that he should, if possible, remain calm and clear-headed."

"You do not take me yet," said Walton, rather distressed that he could not convey what seemed to him so clear; "I should say that such an attitude would give him probably a less rather than a greater clearness of head. But let me finish my explanation. I say that in such a case indifference is impossible; and also it would be not only unnecessary as a safeguard, because his sense of the importance of true knowledge secures him from bias, but would be absolutely an impediment. It would lessen the activity of his mind and the quickness of his perception. It is his sense of danger that prompts him eagerly and carefully to examine all the evidence. Take this away, let him be indifferent, and his motive is gone."

" Oh, of course," Darlington said, " I do not say that he should be indifferent in the sense that he should not realize the importance of the matter; but only that he should still, if possible, examine the evidence impartially, with equal readiness to conclude in favour of either side."

" But what I would have you note," Walton said, " is this; that *very fact*, that makes it all-important to him to *know the truth*, is a fact which makes it impossible for him to do otherwise than wish, and intensely wish, that *one side should prove true rather than the other*. You cannot have the keen personal importance felt without the wish that one side should prove true. The condition, nay, the very reason of that keen personal interest in knowledge of the truth which spurs his mind to active and truth-seeking inquiry, is, in this case, the personal danger involved; and you *cannot* have a keen sense of personal danger without the wish for safety."

" I do not quite see," Darlington said, " that you can bring religious inquiry under these principles. The pressure of immediate personal danger, no doubt, has a great effect in leading the mind to cast aside all prejudice, as the bare pos-

sibility of making a mistake is felt to be far more
serious a consideration than anything else that
there is no temptation to look at anything but
truth. But in religious inquiry there is no such
pressure. The verification is far off and not
under your own control, and a man who is
attached to some form of belief may readily
prefer the indulgence of his hobby to looking
straight at the truth."

Walton began to feel as though it were hopeless
to make his friend keep clearly in mind the real
point of his remarks.

"Why are we still at cross purposes?" he said,
with something of irritation. "I am labouring
to bring home to you that one who has a sense
that a matter concerns him vitally, that one
conclusion means safety, the opposite one danger,
one happiness, the other unhappiness, cannot be
indifferent as to which conclusion the evidence
points to, but has, nevertheless, in his anxiety to
know the truth, an absolute guarantee that he will
be fair-minded; and you reply that men may not
have the sense that the truth of their religion
does concern them vitally. I do not say that all
have. What I do say is that in proportion as

they have it, in the same proportion will they be
sensitive to the happiness of finding a religion
which they love to be true, or to the unhappiness
of finding religious knowledge, which is so much
to them, incapable of attainment. That very
keenness with which they perceive the matter to
be all-important involves a sense as to *why* it is
all-important. It is all-important because it is
bound up with their happiness. And the more
keenly this is felt, the more as a necessary consequence is the conclusion desired which is for
their happiness. I conclude, then, that *this sort*
of wish to believe is only a sign of that keen
interest in the real state of the facts which will
lead to truth, and you reply that a wish to believe
where there is no such keen interest may lead to
error. I state that, where the whole desire is that
good news should be true, it gives an eye for truth ;
and you reply that the wish to indulge a hobby
may lead to error. We are really going back to
the very beginning of all our conversations on the
subject."

Darlington's face did not express precisely
agreement or disagreement, but rather some be-
wilderment in his mind, which might have been

the result of his gradually progressing assimilation
of the ideas which Walton had been setting before
him. Walton at all events interpreted his expression in this sense and was encouraged to
proceed.

"No doubt," he went on, "where the importance of the matter is very immediate, and where
it takes the form of pressing personal danger, my
principle is more apparent; and for this reason,
among others, that the importance of knowing
the truth and the bearing of the facts on oneself
must be felt. A man cannot fail to realise them.
But what I say is just as true in cases where the
importance is not so immediate, provided one takes
the trouble to realise it. There is, I remember, in
Arnold's History of Rome an account of the
attitude of the Roman people when the news of
Hasdrubal's defeat and death at the Metaurus
reached Rome, which will perhaps illustrate what
I have been saying better than so immediate an
instance of personal danger as that of the Czar.
It was, as you remember, an eventful victory, and
involved the destruction of one of the Carthaginian armies. Still it did not decide the war.
Hannibal's army remained untouched, and still

threatened the Romans. Again bear in mind
that Rome was not directly threatened, so that
the personal danger was not so pressing or so
irresistibly forced on the mind as in the other
example I gave. Still the matter concerned the
present and future interests of the Romans sufficiently to make the news of victory very good
news and the news of defeat very bad. They
were so eager, Arnold tells us, to know the true
state of the case that the senate sat from sun-
rise to sunset, and the forum was crowded from
morning to evening, as each hour might bring
the news, and no one could bear to run the chance
of missing it. Then when the first report of the
victory got abroad, far from readily accepting the
evidence, they scrutinised it most closely. 'Men
dared not lightly believe,' he says, 'what they so
much wished to be true.' It was said that two
horsemen of Narnia had ridden home with the
news. But this did not seem sufficient. They
wanted more unexceptionable proof. The truth
of the report seemed liable to objections. 'How,'
they asked, 'could a battle fought in the extremity
of Umbria be heard of two days afterwards at
Rome?' But then came stronger evidence.

A letter was read from Acidinus himself, who
was in command at Narnia, and had heard the
news from the lips of the two horsemen themselves. But many still cavilled at *this* evidence.
The men *might* have been fugitives who trumped
up a tale to hide their own shame. Soon, however, came the news that officers of highest rank
were on their way from the victorious army and
were bringing a despatch from Livius and Nero
the consuls. This seemed more promising, and in
their intense anxiety to learn the true state of the
case they could not quietly await this arrival.
'The whole city poured out to meet them,' says
Arnold. And when at last the despatch had been
read in the senate-house and the forum, and the
facts were conclusively established, they were
welcomed with enthusiasm. A ringing cheer
spread through the ranks of the people, and they
sped to the temples to offer their thanks to the
gods. Now here you have, as it seems to me,
an excellent instance of every point I have urged
on you in these discussions. There is the intense
eagerness to know the truth in so important a
matter, which led the senators to remain all day
in the senate-house and the people in the forum,

and which made them too restless to wait for the consuls' despatch. Then you have the keenly critical examination of the evidence, the readiness to see its weak points, the wish to have it supplemented and confirmed, and throughout the whole story you have as strong a case as can be well imagined of the point on which I have been most recently insisting. Was the attitude of the people in their careful balancing and sifting of the evidence one of judicial impartiality? one of indifference as to whether the evidence proved sufficient or insufficient? On the contrary, the intense sense of the all-importance of the matter which made their investigation so careful and so accurate, contained in it as a part of its essence an intense wish to believe the good news true. Take away this intense wish to believe, and the whole motive power to active inquiry and critical inquiry goes with it. A man who was capable of saying, 'I will look at the evidence with an equal readiness to find the news true or false,' would thereby show that he had none of that sense of the immense importance of the matter which riveted the senators to their seats and crowded the forum, lest one half-hour of absence should lessen their chance of knowing all that was to be known."

Darlington, although now accepting far more nearly than before what Walton had been saying, seemed here again to see a theory, plausible and seemingly true, but which conflicted with acknowledged facts.

"Surely," he said, "you can't and won't deny that, theorise as you may, numbers of men *are* biassed in religious matters by their wishes. Even if you shut your eyes to it in the case of your own co-religionists, you must see it in others. Many a Salvation Army convert, many a Swedenborgian, many a Methodist Ranter, adopts his creed from purely emotional motives. He is hurried on by his wishes. You deal with ideas and not with facts in all that you say."

"I do not deny it," Walton answered. "Even in the case of Catholics I suppose that, naturally speaking, this may happen. All I say is, that to preach indifference as to the result of one's inquiry is to advocate the wrong remedy. The cure for superstition is not indifference but earnestness and seriousness. If I had found, supposing I had been in Rome at the time we have been speaking

of, some man so wrapped up in his own private
studies and theories, and so little realizing the
importance of the matter, that he could, in
judging of the evidence, incline easily towards
the pleasanter side ; that he at once said, before
there was really sufficient evidence, 'Oh yes, I was
sure that Nero would defeat Hasdrubal,' I should
not preach indifference and impartiality as the
best remedy for his unreasonableness.   I should
say, ' Rouse yourself up and realize the importance
of the matter; the good effects of victory, the
evil effects of defeat.'   I should appeal to his own
interest to make him sensible of the reality of the
events that were going on.   ' You are in want of
money.   While the Carthaginian panic lasts no
one will lend it to you.   If this news of victory
be true, you can get it.   Your son wants to sell his
land, but no one will buy it while they fear that
it may be taken from them any day by the invader.
If they advance upon Rome, he has no chance of
selling it.'   I should not be satisfied that he was
in a state to do the fullest justice to the matter
until I had in this way aroused in him a strong
wish to believe the report true, but a wish based on
the thought of facts and consequences, differing

entirely in its character from his previous wish.
If I told him to look at the evidence without bias
merely, true enough, he would not draw a rash
conclusion. But his interest would be dead. He
would not have the motive to seek to know all the
proofs available. He would not go to the forum and
hear Acidinus' letter, or go to meet the messengers
of the consul. If, on the contrary, I make him
realize the importance of the matter, he not only
weighs scrupulously what he has of evidence, but
his intense wish to believe in the good news leads
him to go where he is likely to learn all that is to
be learnt on the subject. And so I say, that to
ask a superstitious man, who has been, as you say,
unduly biassed by his wishes, to look at religious
argument with indifference as to what conclusion
may be true, is to preach the wrong remedy. No
doubt mere impartiality may make him unlearn
a false conclusion, but it cannot bring him to a
true one. I should say to him, on the contrary,
' Realize the gravity of the issue, and that all the
aim of your life depends for its value on the truth
of your creed.' I should endeavour to make him
change one sort of wish to believe for another,—
a light one for a serious one. Then if the creed

he has lightly adopted be true, his sense of the
importance of truth will lead him to examine it
more closely and to see its truth more clearly;
and if it be false, this same sense will make him
sensitive to the weakness and unsatisfactory nature
of his grounds for belief.   It is this realizing of
the importance of knowing the truth that prompts
the search for truth and gives the eye for truth.
I should not pull a man's eye out because
he saw crooked.   I should endeavour to make
him see straight.   The blind man does not see
crooked because he does not see at all.   And
so the indifferent man avoids any admixture of
superstition in his insight into the spiritual world
because he has no insight at all."

"Well then," Darlington said after a pause,
"as I understand you, you would say, applying
your principles to such a case as my own, that if
I look upon the Christian revelation as very good
news if true, and very helpful to me, and very
important, as bearing on my practical life and
future expectations, that state of mind is, if I
realize the gravity of the issue, my best security
for finding out its truth or its falsehood as the
case may be; but that a judicial attitude of mind

is no guarantee that I shall know the full strength of the case. It may lead me to see the weak points and not the strong, whereas the other makes me alive to both. It will secure me against believing without reasons, but will not necessarily lead me to find all the reasons. It will cure superstition, but will not build up religion."

"Yes," said Walton with some hesitation, "that substantially represents what I should say. But you must always keep in mind that it is the sense of the bearing of the facts on yourself which is your great safeguard. I think I may sum the matter up thus:—The rules for judging of evidence on a matter where the *truth* can have no important effect upon oneself one way or another are one class of rules. The mind is viewed in such a case by the philosopher as its physician, and he examines it to see what disease is most likely to creep into it. Take historical evidence, for example. He notes that it is the *decision* on a particular matter, with its links binding it to the various views and historical theories of the inquirer, which is in such a case uppermost in this inquirer's mind ; and he warns him to 'take care not to be filled with the neatness of theories and the symmetry of subjective views. If you want truth, you must view the evidence with no previous bias in favour of this or that theory or view. Such things will sway the mind and tend to make it a little dishonest. The pleasure of consistency, which is tangible and verifiable, is a snare which may entice you from that sobriety of judgment which will land you in unverifiable truth.' But, on the contrary, in a matter of great personal importance, this particular disease cannot attack the mind if that importance is realised. Here it is not the decision, but the *truth* of the decision which is important. No man will indulge a hobby or bask in neat theories if his doing so will cost him his life, or, more truly, no *serious* man will do so. The only danger in such a case is that a man should not be serious. Therefore the philosopher-doctor will say to a man in such circumstances, not ' Be indifferent as to your conclusion,' for he knows that where one conclusion means life and the other death this would be absurd; but, ' Realise the danger, and the importance of knowing the truth, as you have to act on it.' To take a concrete case: suppose it to be a report, with some grounds assigned, that your house is to be broken into by thieves to-night. He will not say, ' Examine the evidence, without a wish to come to one conclusion rather than another,' as this would be absurd and also useless. It would be absurd, because a man by nature prefers safety to danger ; and useless, because fairness of judgment is already ensured by the vast importance of knowing the truth. If it is true, you must take all precautions, send for the police at once, and so forth. He will say rather, suppose he finds you placid and undisturbed, talking of it quietly and giving a list of the reasons for believing and the reasons for disbelieving, ' You do not realize your danger nor the necessity of finding out the truth. If it be true, there is no time to be lost. You must warn the police at once.' The fact that you were indifferent which conclusion the evidence pointed to, would be an infallible sign not of a reasonable frame of mind but of an eminently unreasonable frame of mind. Realize the possible danger, and you at once wish to believe that it is not really existent. The absence of a wish to believe in such a case is an *infallible* sign that you have

P

not the strongest motive power to the discovery
of truth. The keen sense of the personal importance of a matter *must* involve a keen wish. If
knowledge is all that is important, there is the
wish for knowledge. If, as is the case with
most inquiries, one state of facts is looked upon
as good news, another as bad, the more the importance of the matter is felt the greater the
wish to believe in the good news. And in such
a case it is plain that if the keenest sense of its
importance is the best guarantee of thorough
inquiry, the strongest wish to believe will be its
necessary accompaniment. The more the importance of the Metaurus victory was realized, the
more carefully was its evidence scrutinised and
the more intense was the wish to believe it
true.

"Now to apply this in detail, though it is hardly
necessary to do so very fully, to the attitude of
the mind in weighing and investigating the Christian evidences. If they are viewed merely as the
proofs of a past fact, with no personal and present effect on ourselves, then I might allow that,
so far as the historical evidences go, indifference
as to the conclusion to be drawn would be the

best security for their being fairly viewed, not
because it is a supremely good assistant in the
search for truth, but because it is the best one
available under the circumstances. The mind
cannot trust itself to resist the temptation of
building up a theory, neat and satisfying, in harmony with its own preconceptions and prejudices, which may involve a slight deflection
from just judgment, as the fact of the judgment
being absolutely just or no can never be known
by any effect which its true nature will have
on ourselves. The inquirer must therefore constantly ask himself, Am I viewing the matter
impartially, or am I interested—not, be it observed,
in *finding* one particular conclusion to be certainly true, but in deciding for one conclusion
before its truth is ascertained, because it squares
with my theory and so forth? But viewing the evidences as consisting both of internal and external
evidences, of the personal examination of one's
spiritual nature as well as of history, of *à priori*
presumptions, of the necessity for a religion, of
the meaninglessness of life without one, of the
improbability that God, whom we have learnt to
know, would leave us in hopeless darkness, of the

nature of the Christian law and Christ's character
—both felt by meditation and study to be unearthly—of these and the like motives for belief,
added to the historical evidences, and all felt to
converge upon the truth and knowableness of a
fact of supreme present importance to be known,
and calling, if true, for immediate and constant
resulting action, we have quite a different set of
principles to apply. It is both absurd and useless to ask any one who is led to love Christianity
and to see reasons for thinking it not improbable that it may be true, to be indifferent as
to the result of his further study. Absurd,
because if it offers knowledge satisfying his whole
nature, he *must* hope that he shall find it true ;
useless, because if he realises in the supreme importance to himself of a true conclusion, he has
a security for impartiality far higher than that
afforded by indifference."

And now the reader has had a very full account
of Walton's view—indeed Walton has taken
good care that he should know it, and has expressed it very fully. Much to the detriment of
the even balance of the dialogue, and of the
regular alternation of twelve or fifteen lines apiece

which a dialogue with any pretensions to natural-
ness is supposed to have, Walton has, unluckily,
committed an unpardonable breach of such recognised rules. Darlington hadn't his twelve lines
ready, and Walton, whose mind was full of a
subject which had cost him much labour in the
thinking of it out, had scores of lines, all prepared
and waiting to be poured out. Darlington had
been so much occupied with taking in the full
import of what his friend said, and with the
internal confusion in his own mind which had
not yet subsided, that he had not even had a
sufficient sense of propriety to say at the right
intervals, and in default of something better,
" You speak truly, O Walton," or, where he did not
follow him, " Explain to me, O Walton, what is
this you are saying." His mind had, however,
been far from inactive, and although at the time
he would have been unable to give any account
of the effect of the conversation upon him, it
had an effect which became manifest to him by
degrees. Although it is doubtless true that the
set convictions of a thoughtful mind are not
readily touched by argument, still argument felt
to be sound will at least have a considerable effect

on the explanation given of the ground of conviction. And when Darlington had probed the
degree to which Walton's remarks had influenced
him, he found that some such change had taken
place in himself. He was inclined to admit that
he had been inaccurate and too general in supposing that an interest in the truth of a particular
conclusion necessarily implied unreasonable partisanship; he admitted that such a result was not
to be feared where everything depended on the
conclusion drawn being true: further, he was
disposed to allow that, in following up what
appeared a very hopeful clue to knowledge, an
intense desire for knowledge bred a hopefulness
that the clue in question would prove to be a clue
to true knowledge. I do not think that he would
have made an exception of any kind of knowledge
to this rule. He was disposed so far to think
that his own abstract principles had been inaccurate, and that there was a species of "wish to
believe" which was inseparably bound up with
serious reasoning in a matter where one conclusion involves happiness and another unhappiness. Surely then, we are inclined to say, his
convictions must have been modified. If he allowed

that his own attitude in the matter had been
unreasonable, and Walton's reasonable, this must
have considerably shaken his previous views and
theories. And yet the truth is that there was no
radical change in his convictions, and this from
no halting in his reasoning, but from the fact that
in the very act of accepting Walton's analysis he
detected a further consideration in his own mind,
a further element in his own basis of unbelief,
which from the nature of the case Walton was
unable to touch. To put it as shortly as possible,
he saw that a " wish to believe " of the kind fully
explained by Walton was the reasonable attitude
where a really promising clue to knowledge was
found. This seemed plainly true in physical
discovery, and he saw no reason to limit it to this
one branch. He also, though not so readily,
admitted to himself that religion must, if attainable, be a process of individual investigation and
discovery, as appealing to much which a man
must study in his own heart for himself. But
the insertion of one little phrase into his admission
will show how so promising a change of view
collapsed completely so far as immediate change
of conviction went. Darlington would have

inserted between "if" and "attainable" the
words *per impossibile.* That is to say, his original
conclusion dwelt so strong within him as to take
away from his mind the force necessary for actively
applying Walton's principles. A promising clue
which lighted up the mind with the hope of
discovery should indeed give birth to the "wish
to believe," but such a clue he had not found.
Truths about another world and the Author of
our Being were to him too hopelessly beyond the
reach of the human mind to give him any zest in
the inquiry. From several remarks which his
friend made to him in the course of the afternoon, before he left Llandudno, Walton sus-
pected his state of feeling, even before Darlington had expressly acknowledged it to himself.
And he saw that here was a radical defect,
quite outside the reach of all argument. "I
shall pray," he said, "that you may acquire
enough seriousness and a sufficient sense of the
need of religious knowledge and of the import of
that part of your nature which should tell you
that your search for it would not be vain, to
make you work at the matter in earnest. At
present you are stagnant. If your study of

everything else were handicapped by such a state
of mind you would learn nothing. You have no
real wish for knowledge in the matter."

Did Walton think that his conversations with
his friend had been fruitless? No. He was not a
sanguine man as to the immediate result of such
conversations. And he knew well that the initial stage of conversion depends on that grace
which is given as a reward for earnestness, and
which intensifies natural earnestness in its effect.
But he did hold that, once that initial stage was
reached, it was important that a man of active
mind should not be hampered by any feeling
that he might be surrendering to a wholly irrational impulse; and so he was, surprising as it
may seem, not only not disappointed, but pleased
beyond all expectations with the degree of ac-
quiescence which Darlington had ultimately given
to his principles. He looked upon this acquies-
cence as the removal of that very serious obstacle
to the working both of natural reason and of
grace which would have been presented, in case
Darlington should ever be led to look at the
matter in a more hopeful spirit, by the idea
that a longing for belief was unmistakably a

snare and a source of fallacy, and that a state of
calm impartiality was the only safe attitude to be
assumed in such matters. He considered it very
important that the sentimental, irrational, fana-
tical enthusiasm which may lead to the wildest
superstition should be clearly separated in his
mind from all those deeper religious feelings
which give the yearning for true religious
knowledge and the power to gain it; and that
he should clearly see, in case he felt himself influenced by the latter, that the unreason attach-
ing to the former was not to be found *there*. In
order to fix this practical issue in Darlington's
mind, his friend wrote him a letter some weeks
after they had parted company. The following is
an extract from it :—

"We have, then, three attitudes of mind in
religious inquiry. We have first the *superstitious*
attitude, which implies flippancy in belief, readiness in its adoption, equal readiness in changing
it; so slight a depth that belief can hardly be distinguished from imagination, and an easy surrender
to ideas begotten of hope or of fear. Such an
attitude is absolutely unreasonable, and in its most
direct relation to the theme of our discussions it

may lead a man to adopt Christianity from a momentary excitement which its beauty produces in him, his belief having no root, and being unaccompanied by any deep sense of the importance of a true decision. Such an attitude might lead as readily to the grossest superstition as to truth, and it does not seem unreasonable to say that a belief so skin-deep and so lightly assumed could not stand the test of constant action, depending for its worth upon the truth of the creed adopted. We have next the *law-court* attitude of mind—excellent for investigating matters in which the evidence is purely verbal, and which arouse in us a speculative interest only, but in which the true state of the case has no bearing on our own personal welfare. Such an attitude demands absolute impartiality and indifference as to what conclusion the evidence may point to. It is suspicious of any excitement, as experience has shown that excitement in such cases disturbs the reasoning power. It goes on the principle, perfectly sound in such matters, that passion is an opposite force to the love of truth, because passion generally acts in self-interest, and self-interest in such things generally involves prejudice; and so the only way to go safely towards truth is to eliminate passion. This attitude will undoubtedly lead to scepticism, as implying the absence both of fanaticism and of the passion for all knowledge attainable on matters of religion. It will overthrow a false religion, but will fail to find a true. And there is lastly the *religious* attitude of mind properly so called. And this is the attitude for viewing all proofs connected with knowledge which is of vital importance to one's own self. The first essential of this attitude is a deep sense of the importance of the knowledge and of the bearing of the fact to be known upon oneself. This immediately issues in the passion for true knowledge based on this sense, and thus passion is enlisted on the side of reason. And here we must make a distinction. If but two alternatives are before the mind—the sufficiency or insufficiency of a proof explicitly before us, in most cases the fact that the matter is of vital importance will presuppose that one decision is considered to be supremely good news, another supremely bad. This is in most cases the very ground of the all-importance of the matter; and in such cases the intense longing for knowledge is

inseparably bound up with the intense wish to
believe in the happier alternative—a wish making
you as keenly sensitive of its falsehood (if so be)
as of its truth. But viewing religious inquiry as
a whole, not merely as the scrutiny of recognised
verbal evidence, but also as the active search for
all those minute signs of God and of a revelation
which may be found in the human soul and in
the world, the importance of the genuine wish to
believe is shown far more clearly. In this aspect
the wish to believe in any higher and more ennobling form of religion, which manifests itself and
gives good promise of being true, is the concrete
activity of the abstract wish for religious knowledge.
The wish for knowledge gives keen sensitiveness
to every clue, and the wish to believe is the motive
force that follows up the most hopeful clue. Thus
I should say that it would be the abstract wish
for knowledge which would make a mind sensitive
to the *primâ facie* notes of the Church; which
would prevent any unconsciously dishonest blink-
ing of facts telling for her; which would note
with quick eye her works, her system, her actions,
her wisdom, the sanctity of her heroes, until this
general sensitiveness had taken in enough to give

a sense that she offered indeed the most promising clue to knowledge, and then the definite wish to believe would come in. A man who had concluded thus much would proceed then to investigate her more fully, with an earnest desire that what he had been led to look on as a promising source of widest spiritual knowledge, should prove to be such in reality. And I may add that this last aspect of it, viewing, as it does, the wish for knowledge on religious matters as a wish which causes the mind to be keenly sensitive to all clues, and takes the form of the wish to believe when a promising clue is found, seems a far more complete view of the whole question than any which could be gained by confining our view to the looking at particular evidences. This last is indeed only a small part of the whole process, which is analogous, as I have said, to physical discovery rather than to viewing existing verbal evidence alone. There are many rival theories, and of none of them can it be said that the verbal evidence they produce is by itself unmistakably sufficient. Consequently the mode of procedure must be to choose what appears the best, and then to throw oneself into it, and with the hearty wish to find it true and effort to master it, to study its credentials, not in words only, but in all those nameless signs in the religion itself, and in its correspondence with our moral nature, which are quickly noted and taken in by one whose whole heart is in the matter, and which must ultimately, so far as reason goes, turn the balance which was left undecided by the broad aspect of verbal evidence as it existed patent to all alike."

THE END.

PRINTED BY BALLANTYNE, HANSON AND CO.,
EDINBURGH AND LONDON.

A LIST OF

KEGAN PAUL, TRENCH &
PUBLICATIONS.

A LIST OF

KEGAN PAUL, TRENCH & CO.'S

PUBLICATIONS.

CONTENTS.

GENERAL LITERATURE.

A. K. H. B.—From a Quiet Place. A Volume of Sermons. Crown 8vo, 5*s.*

ALLEN, Rev. R., M.A.—Abraham : his Life, Times, and Travels, 3800 years ago. With Map. Second Edition. Post 8vo, 6*s.*

ALLIES, T. W., M.A.—Per Crucem ad Lucem. The Result of a Life. 2 vols. Demy 8vo, 25*s.*

A Life's Decision. Crown 8vo, 7*s.*

ALLNATT, F. J. B., B.D.—The Witness of St. Matthew. An Inquiry into the Sequence of Inspired Thought pervading the First Gospel, and into its Result of Unity, Symmetry, and Completeness, as a Perfect Portrait of the Perfect Man. Crown 8vo, 5*s.*

AMOS, Professor Sheldon. The History and Principles of the Civil Law of Rome. An aid to the Study of Scientific and Comparative Jurisprudence. Demy 8vo, 16*s.*

Ancient and Modern Britons. A Retrospect. 2 vols. Demy 8vo, 24*s.*

ANDERDON, Rev. W. H.—Fasti Apostolici ; a Chronology of the Years between the Ascension of our Lord and the Martyrdom of SS. Peter and Paul. Second Edition. Enlarged. Square 8vo, 5*s*.

Evenings with the Saints. Crown 8vo, 5*s*.

ANDERSON, David.—"Scenes" in the Commons. Crown 8vo, 5*s*.

ARMSTRONG, Richard A., B.A.—Latter-Day Teachers. Six Lectures. Small crown 8vo, 2*s*. 6*d*.

AUBERTIN, J. J.—A Flight to Mexico. With Seven full-page Illustrations and a Railway Map of Mexico. Crown 8vo, 7*s*. 6*d*.

BADGER, George Percy, D.C.L.—An English-Arabic Lexicon. In which the equivalent for English Words and Idiomatic Sentences are rendered into literary and colloquial Arabic. Royal 4to, 80*s*.

BAGEHOT, Walter.—The English Constitution. New and Revised Edition. Crown 8vo, 7*s*. 6*d*.

Lombard Street. A Description of the Money Market. Eighth Edition. Crown 8vo, 7*s*. 6*d*.

Essays on Parliamentary Reform. Crown 8vo, 5*s*.

Some Articles on the Depreciation of Silver, and Topics connected with it. Demy 8vo, 5*s*.

BAGENAL, Philip H.—The American-Irish and their In-fluence on Irish Politics. Crown 8vo, 5*s*.

BAGOT, Alan, C.E.—Accidents in Mines: their Causes and Prevention. Crown 8vo, 6*s*.

The Principles of Colliery Ventilation. Second Edition, greatly enlarged. Crown 8vo, 5*s*.

The Principles of Civil Engineering in Estate Manage-ment. Crown 8vo, 7*s*. 6*d*.

BAKER, Sir Sherston, Bart.—The Laws relating to Quarantine. Crown 8vo, 12*s*. 6*d*.

BALDWIN, Capt. J. H.—The Large and Small Game of Bengal and the North-Western Provinces of India. With 20 Illustrations. New and Cheaper Edition. Small 4to, 10*s*. 6*d*.

BALLIN, Ada S. and F. L.—A Hebrew Grammar. With Exercises selected from the Bible. Crown 8vo, 7*s*. 6*d*.

BARCLAY, Edgar.—Mountain Life in Algeria. With numerous Illustrations by Photogravure. Crown 4to, 10*s*.

BARLOW, James H.—The Ultimatum of Pessimism. An Ethical Study. Demy 8vo, 6*s*.

BARNES, William.—Outlines of Redecraft (Logic). With English Wording. Crown 8vo, 3*s*.

BAUR, Ferdinand, Dr. Ph.—A Philological Introduction to Greek and Latin for Students. Translated and adapted from the German, by C. KEGAN PAUL, M.A., and E. D. STONE, M.A. Third Edition. Crown 8vo, 6*s*.

BELLARS, Rev. W.—The Testimony of Conscience to the Truth and Divine Origin of the Christian Revelation. Burney Prize Essay. Small crown 8vo, 3*s*. 6*d*.

BELLASIS, Edward.—The Money Jar of Plautus at the Oratory School. An Account of the Recent Representation. With Appendix and 16 Illustrations. Small 4to, sewed, 2*s*.

BELLINGHAM, Henry, M.P.—Social Aspects of Catholicism and Protestantism in their Civil Bearing upon Nations. Translated and adapted from the French of M. le BARON DE HAULLEVILLE. With a Preface by His Eminence CARDINAL MANNING. Second and Cheaper Edition. Crown 8vo, 3*s*. 6*d*.

BELLINGHAM, H. Belsches Graham.—Ups and Downs of Spanish Travel. Second Edition. Crown 8vo, 5*s*.

BENN, Alfred W.—The Greek Philosophers. 2 vols. Demy 8vo, 28*s*.

BENT, J. Theodore.—Genoa : How the Republic Rose and Fell. With 18 Illustrations. Demy 8vo, 18*s*.

Bible Folk-Lore. A Study in Comparative Mythology. Crown 8vo, 10*s*. 6*d*.

BIRD, Charles, F.G.S.—Higher Education in Germany and England. Being a brief Practical Account of the Organization and Curriculum of the German Higher Schools. With critical Remarks and Suggestions with reference to those of England. Small crown 8vo, 2*s*. 6*d*.

BLACKLEY, Rev. W. S.—Essays on Pauperism. 16mo. Cloth, 1*s*. 6*d*. ; sewed, 1*s*.

BLECKLY, Henry.—Socrates and the Athenians : An Apology. Crown 8vo, 2*s*. 6*d*.

BLOOMFIELD, The Lady.—Reminiscences of Court and Diplomatic Life. New and Cheaper Edition. With Frontispiece. Crown 8vo, 6*s*.

BLUNT, The Ven. Archdeacon.—The Divine Patriot, and other Sermons. Preached in Scarborough and in Cannes. New and Cheaper Edition. Crown 8vo, 4*s*. 6*d*.

BLUNT, Wilfred S.—The Future of Islam. Crown 8vo, 6*s*.

BODDY, Alexander A.—To Kairwân the Holy. Scenes in Muhammedan Africa. With Route Map, and eight Illustrations by A. F. JACASSEY. Crown 8vo, 6*s*.

BOOLE, Mary.—Symbolical Methods of Study. Crown 8vo, 5*s*.

BOUVERIE-PUSEY, S. E. B.—Permanence and Evolution. An Inquiry into the Supposed Mutability of Animal Types. Crown 8vo, 5s.

BOWEN, H. C., M.A.—Studies in English. For the use of Modern Schools. Seventh Thousand. Small crown 8vo, 1s. 6d.

English Grammar for Beginners. Fcap. 8vo, 1s.

Simple English Poems. English Literature for Junior Classes. In four parts. Parts I., II., and III., 6d. each. Part IV., 1s. Complete, 3s.

BRADLEY, F. H.—The Principles of Logic. Demy 8vo, 16s.

BRIDGETT, Rev. T. E.—History of the Holy Eucharist in Great Britain. 2 vols. Demy 8vo, 18s.

BRODRICK, the Hon. G. C.—Political Studies. Demy 8vo, 14s.

BROOKE, Rev. S. A.—Life and Letters of the Late Rev. F. W. Robertson, M.A. Edited by.

 I. Uniform with Robertson's Sermons. 2 vols. With Steel Portrait. 7s. 6d.
 II. Library Edition. With Portrait. 8vo, 12s.
 III. A Popular Edition. In 1 vol., 8vo, 6s.

The Fight of Faith. Sermons preached on various occasions. Fifth Edition. Crown 8vo, 7s. 6d.

The Spirit of the Christian Life. Third Edition. Crown 8vo, 5s.

Theology in the English Poets.—Cowper, Coleridge, Wordsworth, and Burns. Fifth Edition. Post 8vo, 5s.

Christ in Modern Life. Sixteenth Edition. Crown 8vo, 5s.

Sermons. First Series. Thirteenth Edition. Crown 8vo, 5s.

Sermons. Second Series. Sixth Edition. Crown 8vo, 5s.

BROWN, Rev. J. Baldwin, B.A.—The Higher Life. Its Reality, Experience, and Destiny. Sixth Edition. Crown 8vo, 5s.

Doctrine of Annihilation in the Light of the Gospel of Love. Five Discourses. Fourth Edition. Crown 8vo, 2s. 6d.

The Christian Policy of Life. A Book for Young Men of Business. Third Edition. Crown 8vo, 3s. 6d.

BROWN, S. Borton, B.A.—The Fire Baptism of all Flesh; or, The Coming Spiritual Crisis of the Dispensation. Crown 8vo, 6s.

BROWN, Horatio F.—Life on the Lagoons. With two Illustrations and Map. Crown 8vo, 6s.

BROWNBILL, John.—Principles of English Canon Law. Part I. General Introduction. Crown 8vo, 6s.

BROWNE, W. R.—The Inspiration of the New Testament. With a Preface by the Rev. J. P. Norris, D.D. Fcap. 8vo, 2s. 6d.

BURDETT, Henry C.—Help in Sickness—Where to Go and What to Do. Crown 8vo, 1s. 6d.

Helps to Health. The Habitation—The Nursery—The Schoolroom and—The Person. With a Chapter on Pleasure and Health Resorts. Crown 8vo, 1s. 6d.

BURTON, Mrs. Richard.—The Inner Life of Syria, Palestine, and the Holy Land. Post 8vo, 6s.

BUSBECQ, Ogier Ghiselin de.—His Life and Letters. By CHARLES THORNTON FORSTER, M.A., and F. H. BLACKBURNE DANIELL, M.A. 2 vols. With Frontispieces. Demy 8vo, 24s.

CARPENTER, W. B., LL.D., M.D., F.R.S., etc.—The Principles of Mental Physiology. With their Applications to the Training and Discipline of the Mind, and the Study of its Morbid Conditions. Illustrated. Sixth Edition. 8vo, 12s.

Catholic Dictionary. Containing some Account of the Doctrine, Discipline, Rites, Ceremonies, Councils, and Religious Orders of the Catholic Church. By WILLIAM E. ADDIS and THOMAS ARNOLD, M.A. Second Edition. Demy 8vo, 21s.

CERVANTES.—Journey to Parnassus. Spanish Text, with Translation into English Tercets, Preface, and Illustrative Notes, by JAMES Y. GIBSON. Crown 8vo, 12s.

CHEYNE, Rev. T. K.—The Prophecies of Isaiah. Translated with Critical Notes and Dissertations. 2 vols. Third Edition. Demy 8vo, 25s.

CHICHELE, Mary.—Doing and Undoing. A Story. 1 vol. Crown 8vo.

CLAIRAUT.—Elements of Geometry. Translated by Dr. KAINES. With 145 Figures. Crown 8vo, 4s. 6d.

CLARKE, Rev. Henry James, A.K.C.—The Fundamental Science. Demy 8vo, 10s. 6d.

CLAYDEN, P. W.—Samuel Sharpe. Egyptologist and Translator of the Bible. Crown 8vo, 6s.

CLIFFORD, Samuel.—What Think Ye of the Christ? Crown 8vo, 6s.

CLODD, Edward, F.R.A.S.—The Childhood of the World: a Simple Account of Man in Early Times. Seventh Edition. Crown 8vo, 3s.
    A Special Edition for Schools. 1s.

The Childhood of Religions. Including a Simple Account of the Birth and Growth of Myths and Legends. Eighth Thousand. Crown 8vo, 5s.
    A Special Edition for Schools. 1s. 6d.

Jesus of Nazareth. With a brief sketch of Jewish History to the Time of His Birth. Small crown 8vo, 6s.

COGHLAN, *J. Cole, D.D.*—The Modern Pharisee and other Sermons. Edited by the Very Rev. H. H. Dickinson, D.D., Dean of Chapel Royal, Dublin. New and Cheaper Edition. Crown 8vo, 7*s.* 6*d.*

COLE, *George R. Fitz-Roy.*—The Peruvians at Home. Crown 8vo, 6*s.*

COLERIDGE, *Sara.*—Memoir and Letters of Sara Coleridge. Edited by her Daughter. With Index. Cheap Edition. With Portrait. 7*s.* 6*d.*

Collects Exemplified. Being Illustrations from the Old and New Testaments of the Collects for the Sundays after Trinity. By the Author of "A Commentary on the Epistles and Gospels." Edited by the Rev. JOSEPH JACKSON. Crown 8vo, 5*s.*

CONNELL, *A. K.*—Discontent and Danger in India. Small crown 8vo, 3*s.* 6*d.*

The Economic Revolution of India. Crown 8vo, 4*s.* 6*d.*

CORY, *William.*—A Guide to Modern English History. Part I. —MDCCCXV.-MDCCCXXX. Demy 8vo, 9*s.* Part II.— MDCCCXXX.-MDCCCXXXV., 15*s.*

COTTERILL, *H. B.*—An Introduction to the Study of Poetry. Crown 8vo, 7*s.* 6*d.*

COUTTS, *Francis Burdett Money.*—The Training of the Instinct of Love. With a Preface by the Rev. EDWARD THRING, M.A. Small crown 8vo, 2*s.* 6*d.*

COX, *Rev. Sir George W., M.A., Bart.*—The Mythology of the Aryan Nations. New Edition. Demy 8vo, 16*s.*

Tales of Ancient Greece. New Edition. Small crown 8vo, 6*s.*

A Manual of Mythology in the form of Question and Answer. New Edition. Fcap. 8vo, 3*s.*

An Introduction to the Science of Comparative Mythology and Folk-Lore. Second Edition. Crown 8vo, 7*s.* 6*d.*

COX, *Rev. Sir G. W., M.A., Bart., and JONES, Eustace Hinton.*— Popular Romances of the Middle Ages. Third Edition, in 1 vol. Crown 8vo, 6*s.*

COX, *Rev. Samuel, D.D.*—A Commentary on the Book of Job. With a Translation. Demy 8vo, 15*s.*

Salvator Mundi; or, Is Christ the Saviour of all Men? Ninth Edition. Crown 8vo, 5*s.*

The Larger Hope. A Sequel to "Salvator Mundi." Second Edition. 16mo, 1*s.*

The Genesis of Evil, and other Sermons, mainly expository. Third Edition. Crown 8vo, 6*s.*

Balaam. An Exposition and a Study. Crown 8vo, 5*s.*

Miracles. An Argument and a Challenge. Crown 8vo, 2*s.* 6*d.*

CRAVEN, Mrs.—A Year's Meditations. Crown 8vo, 6s.

CRAWFURD, Oswald.—Portugal, Old and New. With Illustrations and Maps. New and Cheaper Edition. Crown 8vo, 6s.

Crime of Christmas Day. A Tale of the Latin Quarter. By the Author of "My Ducats and my Daughter." 1s.

CROZIER, John Beattie, M.B.—The Religion of the Future. Crown 8vo, 6s.

DANIELL, Clarmont.—The Gold Treasure of India. An Inquiry into its Amount, the Cause of its Accumulation, and the Proper Means of using it as Money. Crown 8vo, 5s.

Danish Parsonage. By an Angler. Crown 8vo, 6s.

Darkness and Dawn : the Peaceful Birth of a New Age. Small crown 8vo, 2s. 6d.

DAVIDSON, Rev. Samuel, D.D., LL.D.—Canon of the Bible : Its Formation, History, and Fluctuations. Third and Revised Edition. Small crown 8vo, 5s.

The Doctrine of Last Things contained in the New Testament compared with the Notions of the Jews and the Statements of Church Creeds. Small crown 8vo, 3s. 6d.

DAVIDSON, Thomas.—The Parthenon Frieze, and other Essays. Crown 8vo, 6s.

DAWSON, Geo., M.A. Prayers, with a Discourse on Prayer. Edited by his Wife. First Series. Eighth Edition. Crown 8vo, 6s.

*** Also a New and Cheaper Edition. Crown 8vo, 3s. 6d.

Prayers, with a Discourse on Prayer. Edited by GEORGE ST. CLAIR. Second Series. Crown 8vo, 6s.

Sermons on Disputed Points and Special Occasions. Edited by his Wife. Fourth Edition. Crown 8vo, 6s.

Sermons on Daily Life and Duty. Edited by his Wife. Fourth Edition. Crown 8vo, 6s.

The Authentic Gospel, and other Sermons. Edited by GEORGE ST. CLAIR. Third Edition. Crown 8vo, 6s.

Three Books of God : Nature, History, and Scripture. Sermons edited by GEORGE ST. CLAIR. Crown 8vo, 6s.

DE JONCOURT, Madame Marie.—Wholesome Cookery. Third Edition. Crown 8vo, 3s. 6d.

DE LONG, Lieut. Com. G. W.—The Voyage of the Jeannette. The Ship and Ice Journals of. Edited by his Wife, EMMA DE LONG. With Portraits, Maps, and many Illustrations on wood and stone. 2 vols. Demy 8vo, 36s.

Democracy in the Old World and the New. By the Author of "The Suez Canal, the Eastern Question, and Abyssinia," etc. Small crown 8vo, 2s. 6d.

DEVEREUX, W. Cope, R.N., F.R.G.S.—Fair Italy, the Riviera, and Monte Carlo. Comprising a Tour through North and South Italy and Sicily, with a short account of Malta. Crown 8vo, 6s.

Doing and Undoing. A Story. By MARY CHICHELE. 1 vol. Crown 8vo.

DOWDEN, Edward, LL.D.—Shakspere : a Critical Study of his Mind and Art. Seventh Edition. Post 8vo, 12s.

Studies in Literature, 1789-1877. Third Edition. Large post 8vo, 6s.

DUFFIELD, A. J.—Don Quixote: his Critics and Commentators. With a brief account of the minor works of MIGUEL DE CERVANTES SAAVEDRA, and a statement of the aim and end of the greatest of them all. A handy book for general readers. Crown 8vo, 3s. 6d.

DU MONCEL, Count.—The Telephone, the Microphone, and the Phonograph. With 74 Illustrations. Second Edition. Small crown 8vo, 5s.

DURUY, Victor.—History of Rome and the Roman People. Edited by Prof. MAHAFFY. With nearly 3000 Illustrations. 4to. Vols. I. II. and III. in 6 parts, 30s. each vol.

EDGEWORTH, F. Y.—Mathematical Psychics. An Essay on the Application of Mathematics to Social Science. Demy 8vo, 7s. 6d.

Educational Code of the Prussian Nation, in its Present Form. In accordance with the Decisions of the Common Provincial Law, and with those of Recent Legislation. Crown 8vo, 2s. 6d.

Education Library. Edited by PHILIP MAGNUS :—

An Introduction to the History of Educational Theories. By OSCAR BROWNING, M.A. Second Edition. 3s. 6d.

Old Greek Education. By the Rev. Prof. MAHAFFY, M.A. Second Edition. 3s. 6d.

School Management. Including a general view of the work of Education, Organization and Discipline. By JOSEPH LANDON. Third Edition. 6s.

Eighteenth Century Essays. Selected and Edited by AUSTIN DOBSON. With a Miniature Frontispiece by R. Caldecott. Parchment Library Edition, 6s. ; vellum, 7s. 6d.

ELSDALE, Henry.—Studies in Tennyson's Idylls. Crown 8vo, 5s.

ELYOT, Sir Thomas.—The Boke named the Gouernour. Edited from the First Edition of 1531 by HENRY HERBERT STEPHEN CROFT, M.A., Barrister-at-Law. 2 vols. Fcap. 4to, 50s.

Emerson's (Ralph Waldo) Life. By OLIVER WENDELL HOLMES. English Copyright Edition. With Portrait. Crown 8vo, 6s.

Enoch the Prophet. The Book of. Archbishop LAURENCE'S Translation, with an Introduction by the Author of "The Evolution of Christianity." Crown 8vo, 5s.

Eranus. A Collection of Exercises in the Alcaic and Sapphic Metres. Edited by F. W. CORNISH, Assistant Master at Eton. Second Edition. Crown 8vo, 2s.

EVANS, Mark.—**The Story of Our Father's Love,** told to Children. Sixth and Cheaper Edition. With Four Illustrations. Fcap. 8vo, 1s. 6d.

"Fan Kwae" at Canton before Treaty Days 1825-1844. By an old Resident. With Frontispiece. Crown 8vo, 5s.

FEIS, Jacob.—**Shakspere and Montaigne.** An Endeavour to Explain the Tendency of Hamlet from Allusions in Contemporary Works. Crown 8vo, 5s.

FLECKER, Rev. Eliezer.—**Scripture Onomatology.** Being Critical Notes on the Septuagint and other Versions. Second Edition. Crown 8vo, 3s. 6d.

FLOREDICE, W. H.—**A Month among the Mere Irish.** Small crown 8vo, 5s.

FOWLE, Rev. T. W.—**The Divine Legation of Christ.** Crown 8vo, 7s.

Frank Leward. Edited by CHARLES BAMPTON. Crown 8vo, 7s. 6d.

FULLER, Rev. Morris.—**The Lord's Day ; or, Christian Sunday.** Its Unity, History, Philosophy, and Perpetual Obligation. Sermons. Demy 8vo, 10s. 6d.

GARDINER, Samuel R., and J. BASS MULLINGER, M.A.—**Introduction to the Study of English History.** Second Edition. Large crown 8vo, 9s.

GARDNER, Dorsey.—**Quatre Bras, Ligny, and Waterloo.** A Narrative of the Campaign in Belgium, 1815. With Maps and Plans. Demy 8vo, 16s.

Genesis in Advance of Present Science. A Critical Investigation of Chapters I.-IX. By a Septuagenarian Beneficed Presbyter. Demy 8vo. 10s. 6d.

GENNA, E.—**Irresponsible Philanthropists.** Being some Chapters on the Employment of Gentlewomen. Small crown 8vo, 2s. 6d.

GEORGE, Henry.—**Progress and Poverty :** An Inquiry into the Causes of Industrial Depressions, and of Increase of Want with Increase of Wealth. The Remedy. Fifth Library Edition. Post 8vo, 7s. 6d. Cabinet Edition. Crown 8vo, 2s. 6d. Also a Cheap Edition. Limp cloth, 1s. 6d. Paper covers, 1s.

GEORGE, *Henry—continued.*

Social Problems. Fourth Thousand. Crown 8vo, 5s. Cheap Edition. Paper covers, 1s.

GIBSON, *James Y.* Journey to Parnassus. Composed by MIGUEL DE CERVANTES SAAVEDRA. Spanish Text, with Translation into English Tercets, Preface, and Illustrative Notes, by. Crown 8vo, 12s.

Glossary of Terms and Phrases. Edited by the Rev. H. PERCY SMITH and others. Medium 8vo, 12s.

GLOVER, *F., M.A.*—Exempla Latina. A First Construing Book, with Short Notes, Lexicon, and an Introduction to the Analysis of Sentences. Second Edition. Fcap. 8vo, 2s.

GOLDSMID, *Sir Francis Henry, Bart., Q.C., M.P.*—Memoir of. With Portrait. Second Edition, Revised. Crown 8vo, 6s.

GOODENOUGH, *Commodore J. G.*—Memoir of, with Extracts from his Letters and Journals. Edited by his Widow. With Steel Engraved Portrait. Third Edition. Crown 8vo, 5s.

GOSSE, *Edmund.*—Studies in the Literature of Northern Europe. New Edition. Large crown 8vo, 6s.

Seventeenth Century Studies. A Contribution to the History of English Poetry. Demy 8vo, 10s. 6d.

GOULD, *Rev. S. Baring, M.A.*—Germany, Present and Past. New and Cheaper Edition. Large crown 8vo, 7s. 6d.

GOWAN, *Major Walter E.*—A. Ivanoff's Russian Grammar. (16th Edition.) Translated, enlarged, and arranged for use of Students of the Russian Language. Demy 8vo, 6s.

GOWER, *Lord Ronald.* My Reminiscences. Cheap Edition. With Portrait. Large crown 8vo, 7s. 6d.

GRAHAM, *William, M.A.*—The Creed of Science, Religious, Moral, and Social. Second Edition, Revised. Crown 8vo, 6s.

GREY, *Rowland.*—In Sunny Switzerland. A Tale of Six Weeks. Small crown 8vo, 5s.

GRIFFITH, *Thomas, A.M.*—The Gospel of the Divine Life: a Study of the Fourth Evangelist. Demy 8vo, 14s.

GRIMLEY, *Rev. H. N., M.A.*—Tremadoc Sermons, chiefly on the Spiritual Body, the Unseen World, and the Divine Humanity. Fourth Edition. Crown 8vo, 6s.

G. S. B.—A Study of the Prologue and Epilogue in English Literature from Shakespeare to Dryden. Crown 8vo, 5s.

GUSTAFSON, *Alex.*—The Foundation of Death. Third Edition. Crown 8vo, 5s.

HAECKEL, Prof. Ernst.—The History of Creation. Translation revised by Professor E. RAY LANKESTER, M.A., F.R.S. With Coloured Plates and Genealogical Trees of the various groups of both Plants and Animals. 2 vols. Third Edition. Post 8vo, 32s.

The History of the Evolution of Man. With numerous Illustrations. 2 vols. Post 8vo, 32s.

A Visit to Ceylon. Post 8vo, 7s. 6d.

Freedom in Science and Teaching. With a Prefatory Note by T. H. HUXLEY, F.R.S. Crown 8vo, 5s.

HALF-CROWN SERIES :—

A Lost Love. By ANNA C. OGLE [Ashford Owen].

Sister Dora : a Biography. By MARGARET LONSDALE.

True Words for Brave Men : a Book for Soldiers and Sailors. By the late CHARLES KINGSLEY.

Notes of Travel : being Extracts from the Journals of Count VON MOLTKE.

English Sonnets. Collected and Arranged by J. DENNIS.

London Lyrics. By F. LOCKER.

Home Songs for Quiet Hours. By the Rev. Canon R. H. BAYNES.

HARRIS, William.—The History of the Radical Party in Parliament. Demy 8vo, 15s.

HARROP, Robert.—Bolingbroke. A Political Study and Criticism. Demy 8vo, 14s.

HART, Rev. J. W. T.—The Autobiography of Judas Iscariot. A Character Study. Crown 8vo, 3s. 6d.

HAWEIS, Rev. H. R., M.A.—Current Coin. Materialism—The Devil—Crime—Drunkenness—Pauperism—Emotion—Recreation—The Sabbath. Fifth Edition. Crown 8vo, 5s.

Arrows in the Air. Fifth Edition. Crown 8vo, 5s.

Speech in Season. Fifth Edition. Crown 8vo, 5s.

Thoughts for the Times. Thirteenth Edition. Crown 8vo, 5s.

Unsectarian Family Prayers. New Edition. Fcap. 8vo, 1s. 6d.

HAWKINS, Edwards Comerford.—Spirit and Form. Sermons preached in the Parish Church of Leatherhead. Crown 8vo, 6s.

HAWTHORNE, Nathaniel.—Works. Complete in Twelve Volumes. Large post 8vo, 7s. 6d. each volume.

VOL. I. TWICE-TOLD TALES.
II. MOSSES FROM AN OLD MANSE.
III. THE HOUSE OF THE SEVEN GABLES, AND THE SNOW IMAGE.

HAWTHORNE, Nathaniel—continued.

VOL. IV. · THE WONDERBOOK, TANGLEWOOD TALES, AND GRAND
FATHER'S CHAIR.

V. THE SCARLET LETTER, AND THE BLITHEDALE ROMANCE.

VI. THE MARBLE FAUN. [Transformation.]

VII. }
VIII. } OUR OLD HOME, AND ENGLISH NOTE-BOOKS.

IX. AMERICAN NOTE-BOOKS.

X. FRENCH AND ITALIAN NOTE-BOOKS.

XI. SEPTIMIUS FELTON, THE DOLLIVER ROMANCE, FANSHAWE,
AND, IN AN APPENDIX, THE ANCESTRAL FOOTSTEP.

XII. TALES AND ESSAYS, AND OTHER PAPERS, WITH A BIO-
GRAPHICAL SKETCH OF HAWTHORNE.

*HAYES, A. A., Junr.—*New Colorado, and the Santa Fé Trail.
With Map and 60 Illustrations. Square 8vo, 9s.

*HENNESSY, Sir John Pope.—*Ralegh in Ireland. With his Letters
on Irish Affairs and some Contemporary Documents. Large crown
8vo, printed on hand-made paper, parchment, 10s. 6d.

*HENRY, Philip.—*Diaries and Letters of. Edited by MATTHEW
HENRY LEE, M.A. Large crown 8vo, 7s. 6d.

*HIDE, Albert.—*The Age to Come. Small crown 8vo, 2s. 6d.

*HIME, Major H. W. L., R.A.—*Wagnerism : A Protest. Crown
8vo, 2s. 6d.

*HINTON, J.—*Life and Letters. With an Introduction by Sir W.
W. GULL, Bart., and Portrait engraved on Steel by C. H. Jeens.
Fifth Edition. Crown 8vo, 8s. 6d.

Philosophy and Religion. Selections from the Manuscripts of
the late James Hinton. Edited by CAROLINE HADDON. Second
Edition. Crown 8vo, 5s.

The Law Breaker, and The Coming of the Law.
Edited by MARGARET HINTON. Crown 8vo, 6s.

The Mystery of Pain. New Edition. Fcap. 8vo, 1s.

Hodson of Hodson's Horse ; or, Twelve Years of a Soldier's Life
in India. Being extracts from the Letters of the late Major
W. S. R. Hodson. With a Vindication from the Attack of Mr.
Bosworth Smith. Edited by his brother, G. H. HODSON, M.A.
Fourth Edition. Large crown 8vo, 5s.

*HOLTHAM, E. G.—*Eight Years in Japan, 1873-1881. Work,
Travel, and Recreation. With three Maps. Large crown 8vo, 9s.

Homology of Economic Justice. An Essay by an East India
Merchant. Small crown 8vo, 5s.

*HOOPER, Mary.—*Little Dinners : How to Serve them with
Elegance and Economy. Eighteenth Edition. Crown
8vo, 2s. 6d.

HOOPER, Mary—continued.

Cookery for Invalids, Persons of Delicate Digestion, and Children. Fourth Edition. Crown 8vo, 2*s.* 6*d.*

Every-Day Meals. Being Economical and Wholesome Recipes for Breakfast, Luncheon, and Supper. Sixth Edition. Crown 8vo, 2*s.* 6*d.*

HOPKINS, Ellice. — **Work amongst Working Men.** Fifth Edition. Crown 8vo, 3*s.* 6*d.*

HOSPITALIER, E.—**The Modern Applications of Electricity.** Translated and Enlarged by JULIUS MAIER, Ph.D. 2 vols. Second Edition, Revised, with many additions and numerous Illustrations. Demy 8vo, 12*s.* 6*d.* each volume.

VOL. I.—Electric Generators, Electric Light.
VOL. II.—Telephone : Various Applications : Electrical Transmission of Energy.

Household Readings on Prophecy. By a Layman. Small crown 8vo, 3*s.* 6*d.*

HUGHES, Henry.—**The Redemption of the World.** Crown 8vo, 3*s.* 6*d.*

HUNTINGFORD, Rev. E., D.C.L.—**The Apocalypse.** With a Commentary and Introductory Essay. Demy 8vo, 5*s.*

HUTCHINSON, H.—**Thought Symbolism, and Grammatic Illusions.** Being a Treatise on the Nature, Purpose and Material of Speech. Crown 8vo, 5*s.*

HUTTON, Rev. C. F.—**Unconscious Testimony ;** or, The Silent Witness of the Hebrew to the Truth of the Historical Scriptures. Crown 8vo, 2*s.* 6*d.*

HYNDMAN, H. M.—**The Historical Basis of Socialism in England.** Large crown 8vo, 8*s.* 6*d.*

IM THURN, Everard F.—**Among the Indians of Guiana.** Being Sketches, chiefly anthropologic, from the Interior of British Guiana. With 53 Illustrations and a Map. Demy 8vo, 18*s.*

JACCOUD, Prof. S.—**The Curability and Treatment of Pulmonary Phthisis.** Translated and edited by MONTAGU LUBBOCK, M.D. Demy 8vo, 15*s.*

Jaunt in a Junk : A Ten Days' Cruise in Indian Seas. Large crown 8vo, 7*s.* 6*d.*

JENKINS, E., and RAYMOND, J.—**The Architect's Legal Handbook.** Third Edition, revised. Crown 8vo, 6*s.*

JENNINGS, Mrs. Vaughan.—**Rahel :** Her Life and Letters. Large crown 8vo, 7*s.* 6*d.*

JERVIS, Rev. W. Henley.—The Gallican Church and the Revolution. A Sequel to the History of the Church of France, from the Concordat of Bologna to the Revolution. Demy 8vo, 18s.

JOEL, L.—A Consul's Manual and Shipowner's and Shipmaster's Practical Guide in their Transactions Abroad. With Definitions of Nautical, Mercantile, and Legal Terms; a Glossary of Mercantile Terms in English, French, German, Italian, and Spanish; Tables of the Money, Weights, and Measures of the Principal Commercial Nations and their Equivalents in British Standards; and Forms of Consular and Notarial Acts. Demy 8vo, 12s.

JOHNSTONE, C. F., M.A.—Historical Abstracts: being Outlines of the History of some of the less known States of Europe. Crown 8vo, 7s. 6d.

JOLLY, William, F.R.S.E., etc.—The Life of John Duncan, Scotch Weaver and Botanist. With Sketches of his Friends and Notices of his Times. Second Edition. Large crown 8vo, with Etched Portrait, 9s.

JONES, C. A.—The Foreign Freaks of Five Friends. With 30 Illustrations. Crown 8vo, 6s.

JOYCE, P. W., LL.D., etc.—Old Celtic Romances. Translated from the Gaelic. Crown 8vo, 7s. 6d.

KAUFMANN, Rev. M., B.A.—Socialism: its Nature, its Dangers, and its Remedies considered. Crown 8vo, 7s. 6d.

Utopias; or, Schemes of Social Improvement, from Sir Thomas More to Karl Marx. Crown 8vo, 5s.

KAY, David, F.R.G.S.—Education and Educators. Crown 8vo, 7s. 6d.

KAY, Joseph.—Free Trade in Land. Edited by his Widow. With Preface by the Right Hon. JOHN BRIGHT, M.P. Seventh Edition. Crown 8vo, 5s.

KEMPIS, Thomas à.—Of the Imitation of Christ. Parchment Library Edition.—Parchment or cloth, 6s.; vellum, 7s. 6d. The Red Line Edition, fcap. 8vo, red edges, 2s. 6d. The Cabinet Edition, small 8vo, cloth limp, 1s.; cloth boards, red edges, 1s. 6d. The Miniature Edition, red edges, 32mo, 1s.

⁎⁎⁎ All the above Editions may be had in various extra bindings.

KENT, C.—Corona Catholica ad Petri successoris Pedes Oblata. De Summi Pontificis Leonis XIII. Assumptione Epigramma. In Quinquaginta Linguis. Fcap. 4to, 15s.

KETTLEWELL, Rev. S.—Thomas à Kempis and the Brothers of Common Life. 2 vols. With Frontispieces. Demy 8vo, 30s.

*** Also an Abridged Edition, in one volume. With Portrait. Crown 8vo, 7s. 6d.

KIDD, Joseph, M.D.—The Laws of Therapeutics ; or, the Science and Art of Medicine. Second Edition. Crown 8vo, 6s.

KINGSFORD, Anna, M.D.—The Perfect Way in Diet. A Treatise advocating a Return to the Natural and Ancient Food of our Race. Small crown 8vo, 2s.

KINGSLEY, Charles, M.A.—Letters and Memories of his Life. Edited by his Wife. With two Steel Engraved Portraits, and Vignettes on Wood. Fifteenth Cabinet Edition. 2 vols. Crown 8vo, 12s.

*** Also a People's Edition, in one volume. With Portrait. Crown 8vo, 6s.

All Saints' Day, and other Sermons. Edited by the Rev. W. HARRISON. Third Edition. Crown 8vo, 7s. 6d.

True Words for Brave Men. A Book for Soldiers' and Sailors' Libraries. Eleventh Edition. Crown 8vo, 2s. 6d.

KNOX, Alexander A.—The New Playground ; or, Wanderings in Algeria. New and Cheaper Edition. Large crown 8vo, 6s.

LANDON, Joseph.—School Management ; Including a General View of the Work of Education, Organization, and Discipline. Third Edition. Crown 8vo, 6s.

LAURIE, S. S.—The Training of Teachers, and other Educational Papers. Crown 8vo, 7s. 6d.

LEE, Rev. F. G., D.C.L.—The Other World ; or, Glimpses of the Supernatural. 2 vols. A New Edition. Crown 8vo, 15s.

Letters from an Unknown Friend. By the Author of " Charles Lowder." With a Preface by the Rev. W. H. CLEAVER. Fcap. 8vo, 1s.

Letters from a Young Emigrant in Manitoba. Second Edition. Small crown 8vo, 3s. 6d.

Leward, Frank. Edited by CHARLES BAMPTON. Crown 8vo, 7s. 6d.

LEWIS, Edward Dillon.—A Draft Code of Criminal Law and Procedure. Demy 8vo, 21s.

LILLIE, Arthur, M.R.A.S.—The Popular Life of Buddha. Containing an Answer to the Hibbert Lectures of 1881. With Illustrations. Crown 8vo, 6s.

LLOYD, Walter.—The Hope of the World : An Essay on Universal Redemption. Crown 8vo, 5s.

LONSDALE, Margaret.—Sister Dora : a Biography. With Portrait. Cheap Edition. Crown 8vo, 2s. 6d.

LOUNSBURY, Thomas R.—James Fenimore Cooper. With Portrait. Crown 8vo, 5*s.*

LOWDER, Charles.—A Biography. By the Author of "St. Teresa." New and Cheaper Edition. Crown 8vo. With Portrait. 3*s.* 6*d.*

LÜCKES, Eva C. E.—Lectures on General Nursing, delivered to the Probationers of the London Hospital Training School for Nurses. Crown 8vo, 2*s.* 6*d.*

LYALL, William Rowe, D.D.—Propædeia Prophetica ; or, The Use and Design of the Old Testament Examined. New Edition. With Notices by GEORGE C. PEARSON, M.A., Hon. Canon of Canterbury. Demy 8vo.

LYTTON, Edward Bulwer, Lord.—Life, Letters and Literary Remains. By his Son, the EARL OF LYTTON. With Portraits, Illustrations and Facsimiles. Demy 8vo. Vols. I. and II., 32*s.*

MACAULAY, G. C.—Francis Beaumont : A Critical Study. Crown 8vo, 5*s.*

MAC CALLUM, M. W.—Studies in Low German and High German Literature. Crown 8vo, 6*s.*

MACHIAVELLI, Niccolò. — Life and Times. By Prof. VILLARI. Translated by LINDA VILLARI. 4 vols. Large post, 8vo, 48*s.*

MACHIAVELLI, Niccolò.—Discourses on the First Decade of Titus Livius. Translated from the Italian by NINIAN HILL THOMSON, M.A. Large crown 8vo, 12*s.*

The Prince. Translated from the Italian by N. H. T. Small crown 8vo, printed on hand-made paper, bevelled boards, 6*s.*

MACKENZIE, Alexander.—How India is Governed. Being an Account of England's Work in India. Small crown 8vo, 2*s.*

MACNAUGHT, Rev. John.—Cœna Domini : An Essay on the Lord's Supper, its Primitive Institution, Apostolic Uses, and Subsequent History. Demy 8vo, 14*s.*

MACWALTER, Rev. G. S.—Life of Antonio Rosmini Serbati (Founder of the Institute of Charity). 2 vols. Demy 8vo. [Vol. I. now ready, price 12*s.*

MAGNUS, Mrs.—About the Jews since Bible Times. From the Babylonian Exile till the English Exodus. Small crown 8vo, 6*s.*

MAIR, R. S., M.D., F.R.C.S.E.—The Medical Guide for Anglo-Indians. Being a Compendium of Advice to Europeans in India, relating to the Preservation and Regulation of Health. With a Supplement on the Management of Children in India. Second Edition. Crown 8vo, limp cloth, 3*s.* 6*d.*

MALDEN, Henry Elliot.—Vienna, 1683. The History and Conse-quences of the Defeat of the Turks before Vienna, September 12th, 1683, by John Sobieski, King of Poland, and Charles Leopold, Duke of Lorraine. Crown 8vo, 4*s.* 6*d.*

c

Many Voices. A volume of Extracts from the Religious Writers of Christendom from the First to the Sixteenth Century. With Biographical Sketches. Crown 8vo, cloth extra, red edges, 6s.

MARKHAM, Capt. Albert Hastings, R.N.—**The Great Frozen Sea :** A Personal Narrative of the Voyage of the *Alert* during the Arctic Expedition of 1875-6. With 6 Full-page Illustrations, 2 Maps, and 27 Woodcuts. Sixth and Cheaper Edition. Crown 8vo, 6s.

A Polar Reconnaissance : being the Voyage of the *Isbjörn* to Novaya Zemlya in 1879. With 10 Illustrations. Demy 8vo, 16s.

Marriage and Maternity ; or, Scripture Wives and Mothers. Small crown 8vo, 4s. 6d.

MARTINEAU, Gertrude.—**Outline Lessons on Morals.** Small crown 8vo, 3s. 6d.

MAUDSLEY, H., M.D.—**Body and Will.** Being an Essay concerning Will, in its Metaphysical, Physiological, and Pathological Aspects. 8vo, 12s.

McGRATH, Terence.—**Pictures from Ireland.** New and Cheaper Edition. Crown 8vo, 2s.

MEREDITH, M.A.—**Theotokos, the Example for Woman.** Dedicated, by permission, to Lady Agnes Wood. Revised by the Venerable Archdeacon DENISON. 32mo, limp cloth, 1s. 6d.

MILLER, Edward.—**The History and Doctrines of Irvingism ;** or, The so-called Catholic and Apostolic Church. 2 vols. Large post 8vo, 25s.

The Church in Relation to the State. Large crown 8vo, 7s. 6d.

MINCHIN, J. G.—**Bulgaria since the War :** Notes of a Tour in the Autumn of 1879. Small crown 8vo, 3s. 6d.

MITCHELL, Lucy M.—**A History of Ancient Sculpture.** With numerous Illustrations, including 6 Plates in Phototype. Super royal 8vo, 42s.

Selections from Ancient Sculpture. Being a Portfolio containing Reproductions in Phototype of 36 Masterpieces of Ancient Art to illustrate Mrs. Mitchell's " History of Ancient Sculpture." 18s.

MITFORD, Bertram.—**Through the Zulu Country.** Its Battle fields and its People. With Five Illustrations. Demy 8vo, 14s.

MOCKLER, E.—**A Grammar of the Baloochee Language,** as it is spoken in Makran (Ancient Gedrosia), in the Persia-Arabic and Roman characters. Fcap. 8vo, 5s.

MOLESWORTH, Rev. W. Nassau, M.A.—**History of the Church of England from 1660.** Large crown 8vo, 7s. 6d.

MORELL, J. R.—Euclid Simplified in Method and Language. Being a Manual of Geometry. Compiled from the most important French Works, approved by the University of Paris and the Minister of Public Instruction. Fcap. 8vo, 2*s.* 6*d.*

MORRIS, George.—The Duality of all Divine Truth in our Lord Jesus Christ. For God's Self-manifestation in the Impartation of the Divine Nature to Man. Large crown 8vo, 7*s.* 6*d.*

MORSE, E. S., Ph.D.—First Book of Zoology. With numerous Illustrations. New and Cheaper Edition. Crown 8vo, 2*s.* 6*d.*

MULL, Mathias.—Paradise Lost. By JOHN MILTON. Books I—VI. The Mutilations of the Text emended, the Punctuation revised, and all collectively presented, with Notes and Preface; also a short Essay on the Intellectual Value of Milton's Works, etc. Demy 8vo, 6*s.*

MURPHY, John Nicholas.—The Chair of Peter; or, The Papacy considered in its Institution, Development, and Organization, and in the Benefits which for over Eighteen Centuries it has conferred on Mankind. Demy 8vo, 18*s.*

Nature's Nursling. A Romance from Real Life. By Lady GERTRUDE STOCK. 3 vols. Crown 8vo, 31*s.* 6*d.*

NELSON, J. H., M.A.—A Prospectus of the Scientific Study of the Hindû Law. Demy 8vo, 9*s.*

NEWMAN, Cardinal.—Characteristics from the Writings of. Being Selections from his various Works. Arranged with the Author's personal Approval. Sixth Edition. With Portrait. Crown 8vo, 6*s.*
  •. A Portrait of Cardinal Newman, mounted for framing, can be had, 2*s.* 6*d.*

NEWMAN, Francis William.—Essays on Diet. Small crown 8vo, cloth limp, 2*s.*

New Truth and the Old Faith: Are they Incompatible? By a Scientific Layman. Demy 8vo, 10*s.* 6*d.*

New Werther. By LOKI. Small crown 8vo, 2*s.* 6*d.*

NICHOLSON, Edward Byron.—The Gospel according to the Hebrews. Its Fragments Translated and Annotated, with a Critical Analysis of the External and Internal Evidence relating to it. Demy 8vo, 9*s.* 6*d.*

A New Commentary on the Gospel according to Matthew. Demy 8vo, 12*s.*

NICOLS, Arthur, F.G.S., F.R.G.S.—Chapters from the Physical History of the Earth: an Introduction to Geology and Palæontology. With numerous Illustrations. Crown 8vo, 5*s.*

NOPS, Marianne.—Class Lessons on Euclid. Part I. containing the First Two Books of the Elements. Crown 8vo, 2*s.* 6*d.*

Nuces: EXERCISES ON THE SYNTAX OF THE PUBLIC SCHOOL LATIN PRIMER. New Edition in Three Parts. Crown 8vo, each 1*s.*
  •. The Three Parts can also be had bound together, 3*s.*

OATES, Frank, F.R.G.S.—**Matabele Land and the Victoria Falls.** A Naturalist's Wanderings in the Interior of South Africa. Edited by C. G. OATES, B.A. With numerous Illustrations and 4 Maps. Demy 8vo, 21*s.*

OGLE, W., M.D., F.R.C.P.—**Aristotle on the Parts of Animals.** Translated, with Introduction and Notes. Royal 8vo, 12*s.* 6*d.*

O'HAGAN, Lord, K.P.—**Occasional Papers and Addresses.** Large crown 8vo, 7*s.* 6*d.*

OKEN, Lorenz, **Life of.** By ALEXANDER ECKER. With Explanatory Notes, Selections from Oken's Correspondence, and Portrait of the Professor. From the German by ALFRED TULK. Crown 8vo, 6*s.*

O'MEARA, Kathleen.—**Frederic Ozanam,** Professor of the Sorbonne : His Life and Work. Second Edition. Crown 8vo, 7*s.* 6*d.*

Henri Perreyve and his Counsels to the Sick. Small crown 8vo, 5*s.*

OSBORNE, Rev. W. A.—**The Revised Version of the New Testament.** A Critical Commentary, with Notes upon the Text. Crown 8vo, 5*s.*

OTTLEY, H. Bickersteth.—**The Great Dilemma.** Christ His Own Witness or His Own Accuser. Six Lectures. Second Edition. Crown 8vo, 3*s.* 6*d.*

Our Public Schools—Eton, Harrow, Winchester, Rugby, Westminster, Marlborough, The Charterhouse. Crown 8vo, 6*s.*

OWEN, F. M.—**John Keats :** a Study. Crown 8vo, 6*s.*

Across the Hills. Small crown 8vo, 1*s.* 6*d.*

OWEN, Rev. Robert, B.D.—**Sanctorale Catholicum ;** or, Book of Saints. With Notes, Critical, Exegetical, and Historical. Demy 8vo, 18*s.*

OXENHAM, Rev. F. Nutcombe.—**What is the Truth as to Everlasting Punishment.** Part II. Being an Historical Inquiry into the Witness and Weight of certain Anti-Origenist Councils. Crown 8vo, 2*s.* 6*d.*

OXONIENSIS.—**Romanism, Protestantism, Anglicanism.** Being a Layman's View of some questions of the Day. Together with Remarks on Dr. Littledale's "Plain Reasons against joining the Church of Rome." Crown 8vo, 3*s.* 6*d.*

PALMER, the late William.—**Notes of a Visit to Russia in 1840-1841.** Selected and arranged by JOHN H. CARDINAL NEWMAN, with portrait. Crown 8vo, 8*s.* 6*d.*

Early Christian Symbolism. A Series of Compositions from Fresco Paintings, Glasses, and Sculptured Sarcophagi. Edited by the Rev. Provost NORTHCOTE, D.D., and the Rev. Canon BROWNLOW, M.A. With Coloured Plates, folio, 42*s.*, or with Plain Plates, folio, 25*s.*

Parchment Library. Choicely Printed on hand-made paper, limp parchment antique or cloth, 6s. ; vellum, 7s. 6d. each volume.

Selections from the Prose Writings of Jonathan Swift. With a Preface and Notes by STANLEY LANE-POOLE and Portrait.

English Sacred Lyrics.

Sir Joshua Reynolds's Discourses. Edited by EDMUND GOSSE.

Selections from Milton's Prose Writings. Edited by ERNEST MYERS.

The Book of Psalms. Translated by the Rev. T. K. CHEYNE, M.A.

The Vicar of Wakefield. With Preface and Notes by AUSTIN DOBSON.

English Comic Dramatists. Edited by OSWALD CRAWFURD.

English Lyrics.

The Sonnets of John Milton. Edited by MARK PATTISON, With Portrait after Vertue.

French Lyrics. Selected and Annotated by GEORGE SAINTS-BURY. With a Miniature Frontispiece designed and etched by H. G. Glindoni.

Fables by Mr. John Gay. With Memoir by AUSTIN DOBSON, and an Etched Portrait from an unfinished Oil Sketch by Sir Godfrey Kneller.

Select Letters of Percy Bysshe Shelley. Edited, with an Introduction, by RICHARD GARNETT.

The Christian Year. Thoughts in Verse for the Sundays and Holy Days throughout the Year. With Miniature Portrait of the Rev. J. Keble, after a Drawing by G. Richmond, R.A.

Shakspere's Works. Complete in Twelve Volumes.

Eighteenth Century Essays. Selected and Edited by AUSTIN DOBSON. With a Miniature Frontispiece by R. Caldecott.

Q. Horati Flacci Opera. Edited by F. A. CORNISH, Assistant Master at Eton. With a Frontispiece after a design by L. Alma Tadema, etched by Leopold Lowenstam.

Edgar Allan Poe's Poems. With an Essay on his Poetry by ANDREW LANG, and a Frontispiece by Linley Sambourne.

Shakspere's Sonnets. Edited by EDWARD DOWDEN. With a Frontispiece etched by Leopold Lowenstam, after the Death Mask.

English Odes. Selected by EDMUND GOSSE. With Frontispiece on India paper by Hamo Thornycroft, A.R.A.

Parchment Library—*continued.*

Of the Imitation of Christ. By Thomas à Kempis. A revised Translation. With Frontispiece on India paper, from a Design by W. B. Richmond.

Poems: Selected from Percy Bysshe Shelley. Dedicated to Lady Shelley. With a Preface by Richard Garnett and a Miniature Frontispiece.

** The above volumes may also be had in a variety of leather bindings.

PARSLOE, Joseph.—Our Railways. Sketches, Historical and Descriptive. With Practical Information as to Fares and Rates, etc., and a Chapter on Railway Reform. Crown 8vo, 6s.

PASCAL, Blaise.—The Thoughts of. Translated from the Text of Auguste Molinier, by C. Kegan Paul. Large crown 8vo, with Frontispiece, printed on hand-made paper, parchment antique, or cloth, 12s. ; vellum, 15s.

PAUL, Alexander.—Short Parliaments. A History of the National Demand for frequent General Elections. Small crown 8vo, 3s. 6d.

PAUL, C. Kegan.—Biographical Sketches. Printed on hand-made paper, bound in buckram. Second Edition. Crown 8vo, 7s. 6d.

PEARSON, Rev. S.—Week-day Living. A Book for Young Men and Women. Second Edition. Crown 8vo, 5s.

PESCHEL, Dr. Oscar.—The Races of Man and their Geographical Distribution. Second Edition. Large crown 8vo, 9s.

PETERS, F. H.—The Nicomachean Ethics of Aristotle. Translated by. Crown 8vo, 6s.

PHIPSON, E.—The Animal Lore of Shakspeare's Time. Including Quadrupeds, Birds, Reptiles, Fish and Insects. Large post 8vo, 9s.

PIDGEON, D.—An Engineer's Holiday ; or, Notes of a Round Trip from Long. 0° to 0°. New and Cheaper Edition. Large crown 8vo, 7s. 6d.

Old World Questions and New World Answers. Large crown 8vo, 7s. 6d.

POE, Edgar Allan.—Works of. With an Introduction and a Memoir by Richard Henry Stoddard. In 6 vols. With Frontispieces and Vignettes. Large crown 8vo, 6s. each.

POPE, J. Buckingham. — Railway Rates and Radical Rule. Trade Questions as Election Tests. Crown 8vo, 2s. 6d.

PRICE, Prof. Bonamy. — Chapters on Practical Political Economy. Being the Substance of Lectures delivered before the University of Oxford. New and Cheaper Edition. Large post 8vo, 5s.

Pulpit Commentary, The. (Old Testament Series.) Edited by the Rev. J. S. EXELL, M.A., and the Rev. Canon H. D. M. SPENCE.

Genesis. By the Rev. T. WHITELAW, M.A. With Homilies by the Very Rev. J. F. MONTGOMERY, D.D., Rev. Prof. R. A. REDFORD, M.A., LL.B., Rev. F. HASTINGS, Rev. W. ROBERTS, M.A. An Introduction to the Study of the Old Testament by the Venerable Archdeacon FARRAR, D.D., F.R.S.; and Introductions to the Pentateuch by the Right Rev. H. COTTERILL, D.D., and Rev. T. WHITELAW, M.A. Eighth Edition. I vol., 15*s*.

Exodus. By the Rev. Canon RAWLINSON. With Homilies by Rev. J. ORR, Rev. D. YOUNG, B.A., Rev. C. A. GOODHART, Rev. J. URQUHART, and the Rev. H. T. ROBJOHNS. Fourth Edition. 2 vols., 18*s*.

Leviticus. By the Rev. Prebendary MEYRICK, M.A. With Introductions by the Rev. R. COLLINS, Rev. Professor A. CAVE, and Homilies by Rev. Prof. REDFORD, LL.B., Rev. J. A. MACDONALD, Rev. W. CLARKSON, B.A., Rev. S. R. ALDRIDGE, LL.B., and Rev. McCHEYNE EDGAR. Fourth Edition. 15*s*.

Numbers. By the Rev. R. WINTERBOTHAM, LL.B. With Homilies by the Rev. Professor W. BINNIE, D.D., Rev. E. S. PROUT, M.A., Rev. D. YOUNG, Rev. J. WAITE, and an Introduction by the Rev. THOMAS WHITELAW, M.A. Fourth Edition. 15*s*.

Deuteronomy. By the Rev. W. L. ALEXANDER, D.D. With Homilies by Rev. C. CLEMANCE, D.D., Rev. J. ORR, B.D., Rev. R. M. EDGAR, M.A., Rev. D. DAVIES, M.A. Third edition. 15*s*.

Joshua. By Rev. J. J. LIAS, M.A. With Homilies by Rev. S. R. ALDRIDGE, LL.B., Rev. R. GLOVER, REV. E. DE PRESSENSÉ, D.D., Rev. J. WAITE, B.A., Rev. W. F. ADENEY, M.A.; and an Introduction by the Rev. A. PLUMMER, M.A. Fifth Edition. 12*s*. 6*d*.

Judges and Ruth. By the Bishop of Bath and Wells, and Rev. J. MORISON, D.D. With Homilies by Rev. A. F. MUIR, M.A., Rev. W. F. ADENEY, M.A., Rev. W. M. STATHAM, and Rev. Professor J. THOMSON, M.A. Fourth Edition. 10*s*. 6*d*.

1 Samuel. By the Very Rev. R. P. SMITH, D.D. With Homilies by Rev. DONALD FRASER, D.D., Rev. Prof. CHAPMAN, and Rev. B. DALE. Sixth Edition. 15*s*.

1 Kings. By the Rev. JOSEPH HAMMOND, LL.B. With Homilies by the Rev. E. DE PRESSENSÉ, D.D., Rev. J. WAITE, B.A., Rev. A. ROWLAND, LL.B., Rev. J. A. MACDONALD, and Rev. J. URQUHART. Fourth Edition. 15*s*.

1 Chronicles. By the Rev. Prof. P. C. BARKER, M.A., LL.B. With Homilies by Rev. Prof. J. R. THOMSON, M.A., Rev. R. TUCK, B.A., Rev. W. CLARKSON, B.A., Rev. F. WHITFIELD, M.A., and Rev. RICHARD GLOVER. 15*s*.

Pulpit Commentary, The—*continued.*

Ezra, Nehemiah, and Esther. By Rev. Canon G. RAWLINSON, M.A. With Homilies by Rev. Prof. J. R. THOMSON, M.A., Rev. Prof. R. A. REDFORD, LL.B., M.A., Rev. W. S. LEWIS, M.A., Rev. J. A. MACDONALD, Rev. A. MACKENNAL, B.A., Rev. W. CLARKSON, B.A., Rev. F. HASTINGS, Rev. W. DINWIDDIE, LL.B., Rev. Prof. ROWLANDS, B.A., Rev. G. WOOD, B.A., Rev. Prof. P. C. BARKER, M.A., LL.B., and the Rev. J. S. EXELL, M.A. Sixth Edition. 1 vol., 12s. 6d.

Jeremiah. (Vol. I.) By the Rev. T. K. CHEYNE, M.A. With Homilies by the Rev. W. F. ADENEY, M.A., Rev. A. F. MUIR, M.A., Rev. S. CONWAY, B.A., Rev. J. WAITE, B.A., and Rev. D. YOUNG, B.A. Second Edition. 15s.

Jeremiah (Vol. II.) and Lamentations. By Rev. T. K. CHEYNE, M.A. With Homilies by Rev. Prof. J. R. THOMSON, M.A., Rev. W. F. ADENEY, M.A., Rev. A. F. MUIR, M.A., Rev. S. CONWAY, B.A., Rev. D. YOUNG, B.A. 15s.

Pulpit Commentary, The. (New Testament Series.)

St. Mark. By Very Rev. E. BICKERSTETH, D.D., Dean of Lichfield. With Homilies by Rev. Prof. THOMSON, M.A., Rev. Prof. GIVEN, M.A., Rev. Prof. JOHNSON, M.A., Rev. A. ROWLAND, B.A., LL.B., Rev. A. MUIR, and Rev. R. GREEN. Fourth Edition. 2 vols., 21s.

The Acts of the Apostles. By the Bishop of Bath and Wells. With Homilies by Rev. Prof. P. C. BARKER, M.A., LL.B., Rev. Prof. E. JOHNSON, M.A., Rev. Prof. R. A. REDFORD, M.A., Rev. R. TUCK, B.A., Rev. W. CLARKSON, B.A. Second Edition. 2 vols., 21s.

1 Corinthians. By the Ven. Archdeacon FARRAR, D.D. With Homilies by Rev. Ex-Chancellor LIPSCOMB, LL.D., Rev. DAVID THOMAS, D.D., Rev. D. FRASER, D.D., Rev. Prof. J. R. THOMSON, M.A., Rev. J. WAITE, B.A., Rev. R. TUCK, B.A., Rev. E. HURNDALL, M.A., and Rev. H. BREMNER, B.D. Second Edition. Price 15s.

PUSEY, *Dr.*—Sermons for the Church's Seasons from Advent to Trinity. Selected from the Published Sermons of the late EDWARD BOUVERIE PUSEY, D.D. Crown 8vo, 5s.

RADCLIFFE, *Frank R. Y.*—The New Politicus. Small crown 8vo, 2s. 6d.

RANKE, *Leopold von.*—Universal History. The oldest Historical Group of Nations and the Greeks. Edited by G. W. PROTHERO. Demy 8vo, 16s.

Realities of the Future Life. Small crown 8vo, 1s. 6d.

RENDELL, *J. M.*—Concise Handbook of the Island of Madeira. With Plan of Funchal and Map of the Island. Fcap. 8vo, 1s. 6d.

REYNOLDS, Rev. J. W.—The Supernatural in Nature. A Verification by Free Use of Science. Third Edition, Revised and Enlarged. Demy 8vo, 14s.

The Mystery of Miracles. Third and Enlarged Edition. Crown 8vo, 6s.

The Mystery of the Universe; Our Common Faith. Demy 8vo, 14s.

RIBOT, Prof. Th.—Heredity: A Psychological Study on its Phenomena, its Laws, its Causes, and its Consequences. Second Edition. Large crown 8vo, 9s.

RIMMER, William, M.D.—Art Anatomy. A Portfolio of 81 Plates. Folio, 70s., nett.

ROBERTSON, The late Rev. F. W., M.A.—Life and Letters of. Edited by the Rev. Stopford Brooke, M.A.

I. Two vols., uniform with the Sermons. With Steel Portrait. Crown 8vo, 7s. 6d.

II. Library Edition, in Demy 8vo, with Portrait. 12s.

III. A Popular Edition, in 1 vol. Crown 8vo, 6s.

Sermons. Four Series. Small crown 8vo, 3s. 6d. each.

The Human Race, and other Sermons. Preached at Cheltenham, Oxford, and Brighton. New and Cheaper Edition. Small crown 8vo, 3s. 6d.

Notes on Genesis. New and Cheaper Edition. Small crown 8vo, 3s. 6d.

Expository Lectures on St. Paul's Epistles to the Corinthians. A New Edition. Small crown 8vo, 5s.

Lectures and Addresses, with other Literary Remains. A New Edition. Small crown 8vo, 5s.

An Analysis of Tennyson's "In Memoriam." (Dedicated by Permission to the Poet-Laureate.) Fcap. 8vo, 2s.

The Education of the Human Race. Translated from the German of Gotthold Ephraim Lessing. Fcap. 8vo, 2s. 6d.

The above Works can also be had, bound in half morocco.

** A Portrait of the late Rev. F. W. Robertson, mounted for framing, can be had, 2s. 6d.

ROMANES, G. J.—Mental Evolution in Animals. With a Posthumous Essay on Instinct by Charles Darwin, F.R.S. Demy 8vo, 12s.

ROSMINI SERBATI, A., Founder of the Institute of Charity. Life. By G. Stuart MacWalter. 2 vols. 8vo.

[Vol. I. now ready, 12s.

Rosmini's Origin of Ideas. Translated from the Fifth Italian Edition of the Nuovo Saggio *Sull' origine delle idee.* 3 vols. Demy 8vo, cloth, 16s. each.

Rosmini's Psychology. 3 vols. Demy 8vo. [Vol. I. now ready, 16s.

Rosmini's Philosophical System. Translated, with a Sketch of the Author's Life, Bibliography, Introduction, and Notes by THOMAS DAVIDSON. Demy 8vo, 16s.

RULE, Martin, M.A.—**The Life and Times of St. Anselm, Archbishop of Canterbury and Primate of the Britains.** 2 vols. Demy 8vo, 32s.

SAMUEL, Sydney M.—**Jewish Life in the East.** Small crown 8vo, 3s. 6d.

SARTORIUS, Ernestine.—**Three Months in the Soudan.** With 11 Full-page Illustrations. Demy 8vo, 14s.

SAYCE, Rev. Archibald Henry.—**Introduction to the Science of Language.** 2 vols. Second Edition. Large post 8vo, 21s.

Scientific Layman. The New Truth and the Old Faith : are they Incompatible? Demy 8vo, 10s. 6d.

SCOONES, W. Baptiste.—**Four Centuries of English Letters :** A Selection of 350 Letters by 150 Writers, from the Period of the Paston Letters to the Present Time. Third Edition. Large crown 8vo, 6s.

SÉE, PROF. GERMAIN.—**Bacillary Phthisis of the Lungs.** Translated and edited for English Practitioners by WILLIAM HENRY WEDDELL, M.R.C.S. Demy 8vo.

SHILLITO, Rev. Joseph.—**Womanhood :** its Duties, Temptations, and Privileges. A Book for Young Women. Third Edition. Crown 8vo, 3s. 6d.

SHIPLEY, Rev. Orby, M.A.—**Principles of the Faith in Relation to Sin.** Topics for Thought in Times of Retreat. Eleven Addresses delivered during a Retreat of Three Days to Persons living in the World. Demy 8vo, 12s.

SIDNEY, Algernon.—**A Review.** By GERTRUDE M. IRELAND BLACK-BURNE. Crown 8vo, 6s.

Sister Augustine, Superior of the Sisters of Charity at the St. Johannis Hospital at Bonn. Authorised Translation by HANS THARAU, from the German "Memorials of AMALIE VON LASAULX." Cheap Edition. Large crown 8vo, 4s. 6d.

SKINNER, James.—**A Memoir.** By the Author of "Charles Lowder." With a Preface by the Rev. Canon CARTER, and Portrait. Large crown, 7s. 6d.

  *** Also a cheap Edition. With Portrait. Crown 8vo, 3s. 6d.

SMITH, Edward, M.D., LL.B., F.R.S. -**Tubercular Consumption in its Early and Remediable Stages.** Second Edition. Crown 8vo, 6s.

SPEDDING, James.—**Reviews and Discussions, Literary, Political, and Historical** not relating to Bacon. Demy 8vo, 12s. 6d.

  Evenings with a Reviewer ; or, Bacon and Macaulay. With a Prefatory Notice by G. S. VENABLES, Q.C. **2 vols.** Demy 8vo, 18s.

STAPFER, Paul.—Shakespeare and Classical Antiquity: Greek and Latin Antiquity as presented in Shakespeare's Plays. Translated by EMILY J. CAREY. Large post 8vo, 12s.

STATHAM, F. Reginald.—Free Thought and Truth Thought. A Contribution to an Existing Argument. Crown 8vo, 6s.

STEVENSON, Rev. W. F.—Hymns for the Church and Home. Selected and Edited by the Rev. W. FLEMING STEVENSON. The Hymn Book consists of Three Parts:—I. For Public Worship.—II. For Family and Private Worship.—III. For Children. SMALL EDITION. Cloth limp, 10d.; cloth boards, 1s. LARGE TYPE EDITION. Cloth limp, 1s. 3d.; cloth boards, 1s. 6d.

Stray Papers on Education, and Scenes from School Life. By B. H. Second Edition. Small crown 8vo, 3s. 6d.

STREATFEILD, Rev. G. S., M.A.—Lincolnshire and the Danes. Large crown 8vo, 7s. 6d.

STRECKER-WISLICENUS.—Organic Chemistry. Translated and Edited, with Extensive Additions, by W. R. HODGKINSON, Ph.D., and A. J. GREENAWAY, F.I.C. Demy 8vo, 21s.

Study of the Prologue and Epilogue in English Literature. From Shakespeare to Dryden. By G. S. B. Crown 8vo, 5s.

SULLY, James, M.A.—Pessimism: a History and a Criticism. Second Edition. Demy 8vo, 14s.

SUTHERST, Thomas.—Death and Disease Behind the Counter. Crown 8vo, 1s. 6d.; sewed, 1s.

SWEDENBORG, Eman.—De Cultu et Amore Dei ubi Agitur de Telluris ortu, Paradiso et Vivario, tum de Primogeniti Seu Adami Nativitate Infantia, et Amore. Crown 8vo, 6s.

SYME, David.—Representative Government in England. Its Faults and Failures. Second Edition. Large crown 8vo, 6s.

Tacitus's Agricola. A Translation. Small crown 8vo, 2s. 6d.

TAYLOR, Rev. Isaac.—The Alphabet. An Account of the Origin and Development of Letters. With numerous Tables and Facsimiles. 2 vols. Demy 8vo, 36s.

TAYLOR, Jeremy.—The Marriage Ring. With Preface, Notes, and Appendices. Edited by FRANCIS BURDETT MONEY COUTTS. Small crown 8vo, 2s. 6d.

TAYLOR, Sedley.—Profit Sharing between Capital and Labour. To which is added a Memorandum on the Industrial Partnership at the Whitwood Collieries, by ARCHIBALD and HENRY BRIGGS, with remarks by SEDLEY TAYLOR. Crown 8vo, 2s. 6d.

Thirty Thousand Thoughts. Edited by the Rev. CANON SPENCE, Rev. J. S. EXELL, and Rev. CHARLES NEIL. 6 vols. Super royal 8vo.
[Vols. I., II., and III. now ready, 16s. each.

THOM, J. Hamilton.—**Laws of Life after the Mind of Christ.** Second Edition. Crown 8vo, 7s. 6d.

THOMSON, J. Turnbull.—**Social Problems; or, An Inquiry into the Laws of Influence.** With Diagrams. Demy 8vo, 10s. 6d.

TIDMAN, Paul F.—**Gold and Silver Money.** Part I.—A Plain Statement. Part II.—Objections Answered. Third Edition. Crown 8vo, 1s.

TIPPLE, Rev. S. A.—**Sunday Mornings at Norwood.** Prayers and Sermons. Crown 8vo, 6s.

TODHUNTER, Dr. J.—**A Study of Shelley.** Crown 8vo, 7s.

TRANT, William.—**Trade Unions: Their Origin, Objects, and Efficacy.** Small crown 8vo, 1s. 6d.; paper covers, 1s.

TREMENHEERE, Hugh Seymour, C.B.—**A Manual of the Principles of Government,** as set forth by the Authorities of Ancient and Modern Times. New and Enlarged Edition. Crown 8vo, 3s. 6d.

TUKE, Daniel Hack, M.D., F.R.C.P.—**Chapters in the History of the Insane in the British Isles.** With Four Illustrations. Large crown 8vo, 12s.

TWINING, Louisa.—**Workhouse Visiting and Management during Twenty-Five Years.** Small crown 8vo, 2s.

TYLER, J.—**The Mystery of Being: or, What Do We Know?** Small crown 8vo, 3s. 6d.

UPTON, Major R. D.—**Gleanings from the Desert of Arabia.** Large post 8vo, 10s. 6d.

VACUUS VIATOR.—**Flying South.** Recollections of France and its Littoral. Small crown 8vo, 3s. 6d.

VAUGHAN, H. Halford.—**New Readings and Renderings of Shakespeare's Tragedies.** 2 vols. Demy 8vo, 25s.

VILLARI, Professor.—**Niccolò Machiavelli and his Times.** Translated by LINDA VILLARI. 4 vols. Large post 8vo, 48s.

VILLIERS, The Right Hon. C. P.—**Free Trade Speeches of.** With Political Memoir. Edited by a Member of the Cobden Club. 2 vols. With Portrait. Demy 8vo, 25s.
₊ People's Edition. 1 vol. Crown 8vo, limp cloth, 2s. 6d.

VOGT, Lieut.-Col. Hermann.—**The Egyptian War of 1882.** A translation. With Map and Plans. Large crown 8vo, 6s.

VOLCKXSOM, E. W. v.—**Catechism of Elementary Modern Chemistry.** Small crown 8vo, 3s.

VYNER, Lady Mary.—Every Day a Portion. Adapted from the Bible and the Prayer Book, for the Private Devotion of those living in Widowhood. Collected and Edited by Lady Mary Vyner. Square crown 8vo, 5s.

WALDSTEIN, Charles, Ph.D.—The Balance of Emotion and Intellect; an Introductory Essay to the Study of Philosophy. Crown 8vo, 6s.

WALLER, Rev. C. B.—The Apocalypse, reviewed under the Light of the Doctrine of the Unfolding Ages, and the Restitution of All Things. Demy 8vo, 12s.

WALPOLE, Chas. George.—A Short History of Ireland from the Earliest Times to the Union with Great Britain. With 5 Maps and Appendices. Second Edition. Crown 8vo, 6s.

WALSHE, Walter Hayle, M.D.—Dramatic Singing Physiologically Estimated. Crown 8vo, 3s. 6d.

WARD, William George, Ph.D.—Essays on the Philosophy of Theism. Edited, with an Introduction, by WILFRID WARD. 2 vols. Demy 8vo, 21s.

WARD, Wilfrid.—The Wish to Believe. A Discussion Concerning the Temper of Mind in which a reasonable Man should undertake Religious Inquiry. Small crown 8vo, 5s.

WEDDERBURN, Sir David, Bart., M.P.—Life of. Compiled from his Journals and Writings by his sister, Mrs. E. H. PERCIVAL. With etched Portrait, and facsimiles of Pencil Sketches. Demy 8vo, 14s.

WEDMORE, Frederick.—The Masters of Genre Painting. With Sixteen Illustrations. Post 8vo, 7s. 6d.

What to Do and How to Do It. A Manual of the Law affecting the Housing and Sanitary Condition of Londoners, with special Reference to the Dwellings of the Poor. Issued by the Sanitary Laws Enforcement Society. Demy 8vo, 1s.

WHEWELL, William, D.D.—His Life and Selections from his Correspondence. By Mrs. STAIR DOUGLAS. With a Portrait from a Painting by Samuel Laurence. Demy 8vo, 21s.

WHITNEY, Prof. William Dwight. — Essentials of English Grammar, for the Use of Schools. Second Edition. Crown 8vo, 3s. 6d.

WILLIAMS, Rowland, D.D.—Psalms, Litanies, Counsels, and Collects for Devout Persons. Edited by his Widow. New and Popular Edition. Crown 8vo, 3s. 6d.

Stray Thoughts Collected from the Writings of the late Rowland Williams, D.D. Edited by his Widow. Crown 8vo, 3s. 6d.

WILSON, Lieut.-Col. C. T. — The Duke of Berwick, Marshal of France, 1702-1734. Demy 8vo, 15s.

WILSON, Mrs. R. F.—The Christian Brothers. Their Origin and Work. With a Sketch of the Life of their Founder, the Ven. JEAN BAPTISTE, de la Salle. Crown 8vo, 6s.

WOLTMANN, Dr. Alfred, and WOERMANN, Dr. Karl.—History of Painting. Edited by SIDNEY COLVIN. Vol. I. Painting in Antiquity and the Middle Ages. With numerous Illustrations. Medium 8vo, 28s. ; bevelled boards, gilt leaves, 30s.

Word was Made Flesh. Short Family Readings on the Epistles for each Sunday of the Christian Year. Demy 8vo, 10s. 6d.

WREN, Sir Christopher.—His Family and His Times. With Original Letters, and a Discourse on Architecture hitherto unpublished. By LUCY PHILLIMORE. Demy 8vo, 10s. 6d.

YOUMANS, Eliza A.—First Book of Botany. Designed to Cultivate the Observing Powers of Children. With 300 Engravings. New and Cheaper Edition. Crown 8vo, 2s. 6d.

YOUMANS, Edward L., M.D.—A Class Book of Chemistry, on the Basis of the New System. With 200 Illustrations. Crown 8vo, 5s.

THE INTERNATIONAL SCIENTIFIC SERIES.

I. Forms of Water: a Familiar Exposition of the Origin and Phenomena of Glaciers. By J. Tyndall, LL.D., F.R.S. With 25 Illustrations. Eighth Edition. Crown 8vo, 5s.

II. Physics and Politics ; or, Thoughts on the Application of the Principles of "Natural Selection" and "Inheritance" to Political Society. By Walter Bagehot. Sixth Edition. Crown 8vo, 4s.

III. Foods. By Edward Smith, M.D., LL.B., F.R.S. With numerous Illustrations. Eighth Edition. Crown 8vo, 5s.

IV. Mind and Body : the Theories of their Relation. By Alexander Bain, LL.D. With Four Illustrations. Seventh Edition. Crown 8vo, 4s.

V. The Study of Sociology. By Herbert Spencer. Eleventh Edition. Crown 8vo, 5s.

VI. On the Conservation of Energy. By Balfour Stewart, M.A., LL.D., F.R.S. With 14 Illustrations. Sixth Edition. Crown 8vo, 5s.

VII. Animal Locomotion ; or Walking, Swimming, and Flying. By J. B. Pettigrew, M.D., F.R.S., etc. With 130 Illustrations. Third Edition. Crown 8vo, 5s.

VIII. Responsibility in Mental Disease. By Henry Maudsley, M.D. Fourth Edition. Crown 8vo, 5s.

IX. **The New Chemistry.** By Professor J. P. Cooke. With 31 Illustrations. Eighth Edition, remodelled and enlarged. Crown 8vo, 5s.

X. **The Science of Law.** By Professor Sheldon Amos. Fifth Edition. Crown 8vo, 5s.

XI. **Animal Mechanism** : a Treatise on Terrestrial and Aerial Locomotion. By Professor E. J. Marey. With 117 Illustrations. Third Edition. Crown 8vo, 5s.

XII. **The Doctrine of Descent and Darwinism.** By Professor Oscar Schmidt. With 26 Illustrations. Sixth Edition. Crown 8vo, 5s.

XIII. **The History of the Conflict between Religion and Science.** By J. W. Draper, M.D., LL.D. Eighteenth Edition. Crown 8vo, 5s.

XIV. **Fungi :** their Nature, Influences, Uses, etc. By M. C. Cooke, M.D., LL.D. Edited by the Rev. M. J. Berkeley, M.A., F.L.S. With numerous Illustrations. Third Edition. Crown 8vo, 5s.

XV. **The Chemical Effects of Light and Photography.** By Dr. Hermann Vogel. Translation thoroughly Revised. With 100 Illustrations. Fourth Edition. Crown 8vo, 5s.

XVI. **The Life and Growth of Language.** By Professor William Dwight Whitney. Fourth Edition. Crown 8vo, 5s.

XVII. **Money and the Mechanism of Exchange.** By W. Stanley Jevons, M.A., F.R.S. Sixth Edition. Crown 8vo, 5s.

XVIII. **The Nature of Light.** With a General Account of Physical Optics. By Dr. Eugene Lommel. With 188 Illustrations and a Table of Spectra in Chromo-lithography. Third Edition. Crown 8vo, 5s.

XIX. **Animal Parasites and Messmates.** By P. J. Van Beneden. With 83 Illustrations. Third Edition. Crown 8vo, 5s.

XX. **Fermentation.** By Professor Schützenberger. With 28 Illustrations. Fourth Edition. Crown 8vo, 5s.

XXI. **The Five Senses of Man.** By Professor Bernstein. With 91 Illustrations. Fourth Edition. Crown 8vo, 5s.

XXII. **The Theory of Sound in its Relation to Music.** By Professor Pietro Blaserna. With numerous Illustrations. Third Edition. Crown 8vo, 5s.

XXIII. **Studies in Spectrum Analysis.** By J. Norman Lockyer, F.R.S. With six photographic Illustrations of Spectra, and numerous engravings on Wood. Third Edition. Crown 8vo, 6s. 6d.

XXIV. **A History of the Growth of the Steam Engine.** By Professor R. H. Thurston. With numerous Illustrations. Third Edition. Crown 8vo, 6s. 6d.

XXV. **Education as a Science.** By Alexander Bain, LL.D. Fourth Edition. Crown 8vo,'5*s.*

XXVI. **The Human Species.** By Professor A. de Quatrefages. Third Edition. Crown 8vo, 5*s.*

XXVII. **Modern Chromatics.** With Applications to Art and Industry. By Ogden N. Rood. With 130 original Illustrations. Second Edition. Crown 8vo, 5*s.*

XXVIII. **The Crayfish :** an Introduction to the Study of Zoology. By Professor T. H. Huxley. With 82 Illustrations. Fourth Edition. Crown 8vo, 5*s.*

XXIX. **The Brain as an Organ of Mind.** By H. Charlton Bastian, M.D. With numerous Illustrations. Third Edition. Crown 8vo, 5*s.*

XXX. **The Atomic Theory.** By Prof. Wurtz. Translated by G. Cleminshaw, F.C.S. Third Edition. Crown 8vo, 5*s.*

XXXI. **The Natural Conditions of Existence as they affect Animal Life.** By Karl Semper. With 2 Maps and 106 Woodcuts. Third Edition. Crown 8vo, 5*s.*

XXXII. **General Physiology of Muscles and Nerves.** By Prof. J. Rosenthal. Third Edition. With Illustrations. Crown 8vo, 5*s.*

XXXIII. **Sight :** an Exposition of the Principles of Monocular and Binocular Vision. By Joseph le Conte, LL.D. Second Edition. With 132 Illustrations. Crown 8vo, 5*s.*

XXXIV. **Illusions :** a Psychological Study. By James Sully. Second Edition. Crown 8vo, 5*s.*

XXXV. **Volcanoes : what they are and what they teach.** By Professor J. W. Judd, F.R.S. With 92 Illustrations on Wood. Third Edition. Crown 8vo, 5*s.*

XXXVI. **Suicide :** an Essay on Comparative Moral Statistics. By Prof. H. Morselli. Second Edition. With Diagrams. Crown 8vo, 5*s.*

XXXVII. **The Brain and its Functions.** By J. Luys. With Illustrations. Second Edition. Crown 8vo, 5*s.*

XXXVIII. **Myth and Science :** an Essay. By Tito Vignoli. Second Edition. Crown 8vo, 5*s.*

XXXIX. **The Sun.** By Professor Young. With Illustrations. Second Edition. Crown 8vo, 5*s.*

XL. **Ants, Bees, and Wasps :** a Record of Observations on the Habits of the Social Hymenoptera. By Sir John Lubbock, Bart., M.P. With 5 Chromo-lithographic Illustrations. Seventh Edition. Crown 8vo, 5*s.*

XLI. **Animal Intelligence.** By G. J. Romanes, LL.D., F.R.S. Third Edition. Crown 8vo, 5*s*.

XLII. **The Concepts and Theories of Modern Physics.** By J. B. Stallo. Third Edition. Crown 8vo, 5*s*.

XLIII. **Diseases of the Memory** ; An Essay in the Positive Psychology. By Prof. Th. Ribot. Second Edition. Crown 8vo, 5*s*.

XLIV. **Man before Metals.** By N. Joly, with 148 Illustrations. Third Edition. Crown 8vo, 5*s*.

XLV. **The Science of Politics.** By Prof. Sheldon Amos. Third Edition. Crown 8vo, 5*s*.

XLVI. **Elementary Meteorology.** By Robert H. Scott. Third Edition. With Numerous Illustrations. Crown 8vo, 5*s*.

XLVII. **The Organs of Speech and their Application in the Formation of Articulate Sounds.** By Georg Hermann Von Meyer. With 47 Woodcuts. Crown 8vo, 5*s*.

XLVIII. **Fallacies.** A View of Logic from the Practical Side. By Alfred Sidgwick. Crown 8vo, 5*s*.

XLIX. **Origin of Cultivated Plants.** By Alphonse de Candolle. Crown 8vo, 5*s*.

L. **Jelly-Fish, Star-Fish, and Sea-Urchins.** Being a Research on Primitive Nervous Systems. By G. J. Romanes. Crown 8vo, 5*s*.

MILITARY WORKS.

BARRINGTON, Capt. J. T.—England on the Defensive ; or, the Problem of Invasion Critically Examined. Large crown 8vo, with Map, 7*s*. 6*d*.

BRACKENBURY, Col. C. B., R.A. — Military Handbooks for Regimental Officers.

I. **Military Sketching and Reconnaissance.** By Col. F. J. Hutchison and Major H. G. MacGregor. Fourth Edition. With 15 Plates. Small crown 8vo, 4*s*.

II. **The Elements of Modern Tactics Practically applied to English Formations.** By Lieut.-Col. Wilkinson Shaw. Fifth Edition. With 25 Plates and Maps. Small crown 8vo, 9*s*.

III. **Field Artillery.** Its Equipment, Organization and Tactics. By Major Sisson C. Pratt, R.A. With 12 Plates. Second Edition. Small crown 8vo, 6*s*.

D

Military Handbooks—*continued.*

    IV. The Elements of Military Administration. First Part : Permanent System of Administration. By Major J. W. Buxton. Small crown 8vo. 7*s.* 6*d.*

    V. Military Law : Its Procedure and Practice. By Major Sisson C. Pratt, R.A. Second Edition. Small crown 8vo, 4*s.* 6*d.*

    VI. Cavalry in Modern War. By Col. F. Chenevix Trench. Small crown 8vo, 6*s.*

    VII. Field Works. Their Technical Construction and Tactical Application. By the Editor, Col. C. B. Brackenbury, R.A. Small crown 8vo.

BROOKE, Major, C. K.—A System of Field Training. Small crown 8vo, cloth limp, 2*s.*

CLERY, C., Lieut.-Col.—Minor Tactics. With 26 Maps and Plans. Sixth and Cheaper Edition, Revised. Crown 8vo, 9*s.*

COLVILE, Lieut.-Col. C. F.—Military Tribunals. Sewed, 2*s.* 6*d.*

CRAUFURD, Capt. H. J.—Suggestions for the Military Training of a Company of Infantry. Crown 8vo, 1*s.* 6*d.*

HARRISON, Lieut.-Col. R.—The Officer's Memorandum Book for Peace and War. Third Edition. Oblong 32mo, roan, with pencil, 3*s.* 6*d.*

Notes on Cavalry Tactics, Organisation, etc. By a Cavalry Officer. With Diagrams. Demy 8vo, 12*s.*

PARR, Capt. H. Hallam, C.M.G.—The Dress, Horses, and Equipment of Infantry and Staff Officers. Crown 8vo, 1*s.*

SCHAW, Col. H.—The Defence and Attack of Positions and Localities. Third Edition, Revised and Corrected. Crown 8vo, 3*s.* 6*d.*

WILKINSON, H. Spenser, Capt. 20th Lancashire R.V.—Citizen Soldiers. Essays towards the Improvement of the Volunteer Force. Crown 8vo, 2*s.* 6*d.*

POETRY.

ADAM OF ST. VICTOR.—The Liturgical Poetry of Adam of St. Victor. From the text of GAUTIER. With Translations into English in the Original Metres, and Short Explanatory Notes, by DIGBY S. WRANGHAM, M.A. 3 vols. Crown 8vo, printed on hand-made paper, boards, 21*s.*

AUCHMUTY, A. C.—Poems of English Heroism : From Brunanburh to Lucknow ; from Athelstan to Albert. Small crown 8vo, 1*s.* 6*d.*

AVIA.—**The Odyssey of Homer.** Done into English Verse by. Fcap. 4to, 15*s.*

BARING, T. C., M.P.—**The Scheme of Epicurus.** A Rendering into English Verse of the Unfinished Poem of Lucretius, entitled "De Rerum Natura." Fcap. 4to, 7*s.*

BARNES, William.—**Poems of Rural Life, in the Dorset Dialect.** New Edition, complete in one vol. Crown 8vo, 8*s.* 6*d.*

BAYNES, Rev. Canon H. R.—**Home Songs for Quiet Hours.** Fourth and Cheaper Edition. Fcap. 8vo, cloth, 2*s.* 6*d.*

BENDALL, Gerard.—**Musa Silvestris.** 16mo, 1*s.* 6*d.*

BEVINGTON, L. S.—**Key Notes.** Small crown 8vo, 5*s.*

BILLSON, C. J.—**The Acharnians of Aristophanes.** Crown 8vo, 3*s.* 6*d.*

BLUNT, Wilfrid Scawen. — **The Wind and the Whirlwind.** Demy 8vo, 1*s.* 6*d.*

BOWEN, H. C., M.A.—**Simple English Poems.** English Literature for Junior Classes. In Four Parts. Parts I., II., and III., 6*d.* each, and Part IV., 1*s.* Complete, 3*s.*

BRASHER, Alfred.—**Sophia ;** or, the Viceroy of Valencia. A Comedy in Five Acts, founded on a Story in Scarron. Small crown 8vo, 2*s.* 6*d.*

BRYANT, W. C.—**Poems.** Cheap Edition, with Frontispiece. Small crown 8vo, 3*s.* 6*d.*

BYRNNE, E. Fairfax.—**Milicent :** a Poem. Small crown 8vo, 6*s.*

CAILLARD, Emma Marie.—**Charlotte Corday,** and other Poems. Small crown 8vo, 3*s.* 6*d.*

Calderon's Dramas : the Wonder-Working Magician — Life is a Dream—the Purgatory of St. Patrick. Translated by DENIS FLORENCE MACCARTHY. Post 8vo, 10*s.*

Camoens Lusiads. — Portuguese Text, with Translation by J. J. AUBERTIN. Second Edition. 2 vols. Crown 8vo, 12*s.*

CAMPBELL, Lewis.—**Sophocles.** The Seven Plays in English Verse. Crown 8vo, 7*s.* 6*d.*

Castilian Brothers (The), Chateaubriant, Waldemar : Three Tragedies ; and **The Rose of Sicily :** a Drama. By the Author of "Ginevra," etc. Crown 8vo, 6*s.*

Christian (Owen) Poems. Small crown 8vo, 2*s.* 6*d.*

Chronicles of Christopher Columbus. A Poem in 12 Cantos. By M. D. C. Crown 8vo, 7*s.* 6*d.*

CLARKE, Mary Cowden.—Honey from the Weed. Verses. Crown 8vo, 7s.

Cosmo de Medici; The False One; Agramont and Beaumont: Three Tragedies; and The Deformed: a Dramatic Sketch. By the Author of "Ginevra," etc., etc. Crown 8vo, 5s.

COXHEAD, Ethel.—Birds and Babies. Imp. 16mo. With 33 Illustrations. Gilt, 2s. 6d.

David Rizzio, Bothwell, and the Witch Lady: Three Tragedies. By the author of "Ginevra," etc. Crown 8vo, 6s.

DAVIE, G. S., M.D.—The Garden of Fragrance. Being a complete translation of the Bostán of Sádi from the original Persian into English Verse. Crown 8vo, 7s. 6d.

DAVIES, T. Hart.—Catullus. Translated into English Verse. Crown 8vo, 6s.

DENNIS, J.—English Sonnets. Collected and Arranged by. Small crown 8vo, 2s. 6d.

DE VERE, Aubrey.—Poetical Works.

I. THE SEARCH AFTER PROSERPINE, etc. 6s.
II. THE LEGENDS OF ST. PATRICK, etc. 6s.
III. ALEXANDER THE GREAT, etc. 6s.

The Foray of Queen Meave, and other Legends of Ireland's Heroic Age. Small crown 8vo, 5s.

Legends of the Saxon Saints. Small crown 8vo, 6s.

DILLON, Arthur.—River Songs and other Poems. With 13 autotype Illustrations from designs by Margery May. Fcap. 4to, cloth extra, gilt leaves, 10s. 6d.

DOBELL, Mrs. Horace.—Ethelstone, Eveline, and other Poems. Crown 8vo, 6s.

DOBSON, Austin.—Old World Idylls and other Verses. Fourth Edition. 18mo, cloth extra, gilt tops, 6s.

DOMET, Alfred.—Ranolf and Amohia. A Dream of Two Lives. New Edition, Revised. 2 vols. Crown 8vo, 12s.

Dorothy: a Country Story in Elegiac Verse. With Preface. Demy 8vo, 5s.

DOWDEN, Edward, LL.D.—Shakspere's Sonnets. With Introduction and Notes. Large post 8vo, 7s. 6d.

DUTT, Toru.—A Sheaf Gleaned in French Fields. New Edition. Demy 8vo, 10s. 6d.

EDMONDS, E. M.—Hesperas. Rhythm and Rhyme. Crown 8vo, 4s.

EDWARDS, Miss Betham.—Poems. Small crown 8vo, 3s. 6d.

ELDRYTH, Maud.—**Margaret,** and other Poems. Small crown 8vo, 3*s.* 6*d.*

All Soul's Eve, "No God," and other Poems. Fcap. 8vo, 3*s.* 6*d.*

ELLIOTT, Ebenezer, The Corn Law Rhymer.—**Poems.** Edited by his son, the Rev. EDWIN ELLIOTT, of St. John's, Antigua. 2 vols. Crown 8vo, 18*s.*

English Verse. Edited by W. J. LINTON and R. H. STODDARD. 5 vols. Crown 8vo, cloth, 5*s.* each.
   I. CHAUCER TO BURNS.
   II. TRANSLATIONS.
   III. LYRICS OF THE NINETEENTH CENTURY.
   IV. DRAMATIC SCENES AND CHARACTERS.
   V. BALLADS AND ROMANCES.

ENIS.—**Gathered Leaves.** Small crown 8vo.

EVANS, Anne.—**Poems and Music.** With Memorial Preface by ANN THACKERAY RITCHIE. Large crown 8vo, 7*s.*

FORSTER, the late William.—**Midas.** Crown 8vo, 5*s.*

GINNER, Isaac B.—**The Death of Otho,** and other Poems. Small crown 8vo, 5*s.*

GOODCHILD, John A.—**Somnia Medici.** Small crown 8vo, 5*s.*

GOSSE, Edmund W.—**New Poems.** Crown 8vo, 7*s.* 6*d.*

GRAHAM, William. **Two Fancies,** and other Poems. Crown 8vo, 5*s.*

GRINDROD, Charles. **Plays from English History.** Crown 8vo, 7*s.* 6*d.*

   The Stranger's Story, and his Poem, The Lament of Love : An Episode of the Malvern Hills. Small crown 8vo, 2*s.* 6*d.*

GURNEY, Rev. Alfred.—**The Vision of the Eucharist,** and other Poems. Crown 8vo, 5*s.*

   A Christmas Faggot. Small crown 8vo, 5*s.*

HELLON, H. G.—**Daphnis :** a Pastoral Poem. Small crown 8vo, 3*s.* 6*d.*

HENRY, Daniel, Junr.—**Under a Fool's Cap.** Songs. Crown 8vo, cloth, bevelled boards, 5*s.*

Herman Waldgrave : a Life's Drama. By the Author of "Ginevra," etc. Crown 8vo, 6*s.*

HEYWOOD, J. C.—**Herodias,** a Dramatic Poem. New Edition, Revised. Small crown 8vo, 5*s.*

HICKEY, E. H.—**A Sculptor,** and other Poems. Small crown 8vo, 5*s.*

HONEYWOOD, Patty.—Poems. Dedicated (by permission) to Lord Wolseley, G.C.B., etc. Small crown 8vo, 2s. 6d.

JENKINS, Rev. Canon.—Alfonso Petrucci, Cardinal and Conspirator: an Historical Tragedy in Five Acts. Small crown 8vo, 3s. 6d.

JOHNSON, Ernle S. W.—Ilaria, and other Poems. Small crown 8vo, 3s. 6d.

KEATS, John.—Poetical Works. Edited by W. T. ARNOLD. Large crown 8vo, choicely printed on hand-made paper, with Portrait in *eau-forte.* Parchment or cloth, 12s. ; vellum, 15s.

KENNEDY, Captain A. W. M. Clark.—Robert the Bruce. A Poem: Historical and Romantic. With Three Illustrations by James Faed, Jun. Printed on hand-made paper, parchment, bevelled boards, crown 8vo, 10s. 6d.

KING, Edward.—Echoes from the Orient. With Miscellaneous Poems. Small crown 8vo, 3s. 6d.

KING, Mrs. Hamilton.—The Disciples. Sixth Edition, with Portrait and Notes. Crown 8vo, 5s.

　　A Book of Dreams. Crown 8vo, 3s. 6d.

KNOX, The Hon. Mrs. O. N.—Four Pictures from a Life, and other Poems. Small crown 8vo, 3s. 6d.

LANG, A.—XXXII Ballades in Blue China. Elzevir 8vo, parchment, 5s.

　　Rhymes à la Mode. With Frontispiece by E. A. Abbey. 18mo, gilt tops, 5s.

LAWSON, Right Hon. Mr. Justice.—Hymni Usitati Latine Redditi : with other Verses. Small 8vo, parchment, 5s.

Lessing's Nathan the Wise. Translated by EUSTACE K. CORBETT. Crown 8vo, 6s.

Life Thoughts. Small crown 8vo, 2s. 6d.

Living English Poets MDCCCLXXXII. With Frontispiece by Walter Crane. Second Edition. Large crown 8vo. Printed on hand-made paper. Parchment or cloth, 12s. ; vellum, 15s.

LOCKER, F.—London Lyrics. New Edition. With Portrait, 18mo. Cloth extra, gilt tops, 5s.

Love in Idleness. A Volume of Poems. With an Etching by W. B. Scott. Small crown 8vo, 5s.

Love Sonnets of Proteus. With Frontispiece by the Author. Elzevir 8vo, 5s.

LUMSDEN, Lieut.-Col. H. W.—Beowulf : an Old English Poem. Translated into Modern Rhymes. Second and Revised Edition. Small crown 8vo, 5s.

Lyre and Star. Poems by the Author of "Ginevra," etc. Crown 8vo, 5s.

MACGREGOR, Duncan.—**Clouds and Sunlight.** Poems. Small crown 8vo, 5s.

MAGNUSSON, Eirikr, M.A., and PALMER, E. H., M.A.—Johan Ludvig Runeberg's Lyrical Songs, Idylls, and Epigrams. Fcap. 8vo, 5s.

M.D.C.—**Chronicles of Christopher Columbus.** A Poem in Twelve Cantos. Crown 8vo, 7s. 6d.

MEREDITH, Owen [The Earl of Lytton].—**Lucile.** New Edition. With 32 Illustrations. 16mo, 3s. 6d. Cloth extra, gilt edges, 4s. 6d.

MORRIS, Lewis.—**Poetical Works of.** New and Cheaper Editions, with Portrait. Complete in 3 vols., 5s. each.
Vol. I. contains "Songs of Two Worlds." Eleventh Edition.
Vol. II. contains "The Epic of Hades." Eighteenth Edition.
Vol. III. contains "Gwen" and "The Ode of Life." Sixth Edition.

The Epic of Hades. With 16 Autotype Illustrations, after the Drawings of the late George R. Chapman. 4to, cloth extra, gilt leaves, 21s.

The Epic of Hades. Presentation Edition. 4to, cloth extra, gilt leaves, 10s. 6d.

Songs Unsung. Fourth Edition. Fcap. 8vo, 6s.

The Lewis Morris Birthday Book. Edited by S. S. COPE-MAN, with Frontispiece after a Design by the late George R. Chapman. 32mo, cloth extra, gilt edges, 2s.; cloth limp, 1s. 6d.

MORSHEAD, E. D. A.—**The House of Atreus.** Being the Agamemnon, Libation-Bearers, and Furies of Æschylus. Translated into English Verse. Crown 8vo, 7s.

The Suppliant Maidens of Æschylus. Crown 8vo, 3s. 6d.

NADEN, Constance W.—**Songs and Sonnets of Spring Time.** Small crown 8vo, 5s.

NEWELL, E. J.—**The Sorrows of Simona and Lyrical Verses.** Small crown 8vo, 3s. 6d.

NOEL, The Hon. Roden.—**A Little Child's Monument.** Third Edition. Small crown 8vo, 3s. 6d.

The Red Flag, and other Poems. New Edition. Small crown 8vo, 6s.

O'HAGAN, John.—**The Song of Roland.** Translated into English Verse. New and Cheaper Edition. Crown 8vo, 5s.

PFEIFFER, Emily.—**The Rhyme of the Lady of the Rock, and How it Grew.** Small crown 8vo, 3s. 6d.

PFEIFFER, Emily—continued.

Gerard's Monument, and other Poems. Second Edition. Crown 8vo, 6s.

Under the Aspens: Lyrical and Dramatic. With Portrait. Crown 8vo, 6s.

PIATT, J. J.—**Idyls and Lyrics of the Ohio Valley.** Crown 8vo, 5s.

RAFFALOVICH, Mark André. — **Cyril and Lionel,** and other Poems. A volume of Sentimental Studies. Small crown 8vo, 3s. 6d.

Rare Poems of the 16th and 17th Centuries. Edited W. J. LINTON. Crown 8vo, 5s.

RHOADES, James.—**The Georgics of Virgil.** Translated into English Verse. Small crown 8vo, 5s.

ROBINSON, A. Mary F.—**A Handful of Honeysuckle.** Fcap. 8vo, 3s. 6d.

The Crowned Hippolytus. Translated from Euripides. With New Poems. Small crown 8vo, 5s.

ROUS, Lieut.-Col.—**Conradin.** Small crown 8vo, 2s.

Schiller's Mary Stuart. German Text, with English Translation on opposite page by LEEDHAM WHITE. Crown 8vo, 6s.

SCOTT, E. J. L.—**The Eclogues of Virgil.**—Translated into English Verse. Small crown 8vo, 3s. 6d.

SCOTT, George F. E.—**Theodora and other Poems.** Small crown 8vo, 3s. 6d.

SEAL, W. H.—**Ione,** and other Poems. Second and Cheaper Edition, revised, crown 8vo, 3s. 6d.

SELKIRK, J. B.—**Poems.** Crown 8vo, 7s. 6d.

SHARP, William.—**Euphrenia:** or, The Test of Love. A Poem. Crown 8vo, 5s.

SKINNER, H. J.—**The Lily of the Lyn,** and other Poems. Small crown 8vo, 3s. 6d.

SLADEN, Douglas B.—**Frithjof and Ingebjorg,** and other Poems. Small crown 8vo, 5s.

SMITH, J. W. Gilbart.—**The Loves of Vandyck.** A Tale of Genoa. Small crown 8vo, 2s. 6d.

The Log o' the "Norseman." Small crown 8vo, 5s.

Sophocles: The Seven Plays in English Verse. Translated by LEWIS CAMPBELL. Crown 8vo, 7s. 6d.

SPICER, Henry.—Haska : a Drama in Three Acts (as represented at the Theatre Royal, Drury Lane, March 10th, 1877). Third Edition. Crown 8vo, 3*s.* 6*d.*

SYMONDS, John Addington.—Vagabunduli Libellus. Crown 8vo, 6*s.*

Tares. Crown 8vo, 1*s.* 6*d.*

Tasso's Jerusalem Delivered. Translated by Sir JOHN KINGSTON JAMES, Bart. Two Volumes. Printed on hand-made paper, parchment, bevelled boards. Large crown 8vo, 21*s.*

TAYLOR, Sir H.—Works. Complete in Five Volumes. Crown 8vo, 30*s.*

Philip Van Artevelde. Fcap. 8vo, 3*s.* 6*d.*

The Virgin Widow, etc. Fcap. 8vo, 3*s.* 6*d.*

The Statesman. Fcap. 8vo, 3*s.* 6*d.*

TAYLOR, Augustus.—Poems. Fcap. 8vo, 5*s.*

TAYLOR, Margaret Scott.—"Boys Together," and other Poems. Small crown 8vo, 6*s.*

THORNTON, L. M.—The Son of Shelomith. Small crown 8vo, 3*s.* 6*d.*

TODHUNTER, Dr. J.—Laurella, and other Poems. Crown 8vo, 6*s.* 6*d.*

Forest Songs. Small crown 8vo, 3*s.* 6*d.*

The True Tragedy of Rienzi : a Drama. 3*s.* 6*d.*

Alcestis : a Dramatic Poem. Extra fcap. 8vo, 5*s.*

TYLER, M. C.—Anne Boleyn. A Tragedy in Six Acts. Small crown 8vo, 2*s.* 6*d.*

WALTERS, Sophia Lydia.—A Dreamer's Sketch Book. With 21 Illustrations by Percival Skelton, R. P. Leitch, W. H. J. Boot, and T. R. Pritchett. Engraved by J. D. Cooper. Fcap. 4to, 12*s.* 6*d.*

Wandering Echoes.—By J. E. D. G. In Four Parts. Small crown 8vo, 5*s.*

WATTS, Alaric Alfred and Anna Mary Howitt.—Aurora. A Medley of Verse. Fcap. 8vo, bevelled boards, 5*s.*

WEBSTER, Augusta.—In a Day : a Drama. Small crown 8vo, 2*s.* 6*d.*

Disguises : a Drama. Small crown 8vo, 5*s.*

Wet Days. By a Farmer. Small crown 8vo, 6*s.*

WILLIAMS, J.—A Story of Three Years, and other Poems. Small crown 8vo, 3*s.* 6*d.*

Wordsworth Birthday Book, The. Edited by ADELAIDE and VIOLET WORDSWORTH. 32mo, limp cloth, 1*s.* 6*d.* ; cloth extra, 2*s.*

YOUNGMAN, Thomas George.—Poems. Small crown 8vo, 5*s.*

YOUNGS, Ella Sharpe.—**Paphus,** and other Poems. Small crown 8vo, 3*s.* 6*d.*

A Heart's Life, Sarpedon, and other Poems. Small crown 8vo, 3*s.* 6*d.*

WORKS OF FICTION IN ONE VOLUME.

BANKS, Mrs. G. L.—**God's Providence House.** New Edition. Crown 8vo, 3*s.* 6*d.*

HUNTER, Hay.—**The Crime of Christmas Day.** A Tale of the Latin Quarter. By the Author of "My Ducats and my Daughter." 1*s.*

HUNTER, Hay, and WHYTE, Walter.—**My Ducats and My Daughter.** New and Cheaper Edition. With Frontispiece. Crown 8vo, 6*s.*

INGELOW, Jean.—**Off the Skelligs :** a Novel. With Frontispiece. Second Edition. Crown 8vo, 6*s.*

KIELLAND, Alexander.—**Garman and Worse.** A Norwegian Novel. Authorized Translation, by W. W. Kettlewell. Crown 8vo, 6*s.*

MACDONALD, G.—**Donal Grant.** A Novel. New and Cheaper Edition. With Frontispiece. Crown 8vo, 6*s.*

Castle Warlock. A Novel. New and Cheaper Edition. Crown 8vo, 6*s.*

Malcolm. With Portrait of the Author engraved on Steel. Sixth Edition. Crown 8vo, 6*s.*

The Marquis of Lossie. Fifth Edition. With Frontispiece. Crown 8vo, 6*s.*

St. George and St. Michael. Fourth Edition. With Frontispiece. Crown 8vo, 6*s.*

PALGRAVE, W. Gifford.—**Hermann Agha :** an Eastern Narrative. Third Edition. Crown 8vo, 6*s.*

SHAW, Flora L.—**Castle Blair ;** a Story of Youthful Days. New and Cheaper Edition. Crown 8vo, 3*s.* 6*d.*

STRETTON, Hesba.—**Through a Needle's Eye :** a Story. New and Cheaper Edition, with Frontispiece. Crown 8vo, 6*s.*

TAYLOR, Col. Meadows, C.S.I., M.R.I.A.—**Seeta :** a Novel. New and Cheaper Edition. With Frontispiece. Crown 8vo, 6*s.*

Tippoo Sultaun : a Tale of the Mysore War. New Edition, with Frontispiece. Crown 8vo, 6*s.*

Ralph Darnell. New and Cheaper Edition. With Frontispiece. Crown 8vo, 6*s.*

TAYLOR, Col. Meadows, C.S.I., M.R.I.A.—continued.

A Noble Queen. New and Cheaper Edition. With Frontispiece. Crown 8vo, 6s.

The Confessions of a Thug. Crown 8vo, 6s.

Tara : a Mahratta Tale. Crown 8vo, 6s.

Within Sound of the Sea. New and Cheaper Edition, with Frontispiece. Crown 8vo, 6s.

BOOKS FOR THE YOUNG.

Brave Men's Footsteps. A Book of Example and Anecdote for Young People. By the Editor of "Men who have Risen." With 4 Illustrations by C. Doyle. Eighth Edition. Crown 8vo, 3s. 6d.

COXHEAD, Ethel.—**Birds and Babies.** Imp. 16mo. With 33 Illustrations. Cloth gilt, 2s. 6d.

DAVIES, G. Christopher.—**Rambles and Adventures of our School Field Club.** With 4 Illustrations. New and Cheaper Edition. Crown 8vo, 3s. 6d.

EDMONDS, Herbert.—**Well Spent Lives :** a Series of Modern Biographies. New and Cheaper Edition. Crown 8vo, 3s. 6d.

EVANS, Mark.—**The Story of our Father's Love,** told to Children. Sixth and Cheaper Edition of Theology for Children. With 4 Illustrations. Fcap. 8vo, 1s. 6d.

JOHNSON, Virginia W.—**The Catskill Fairies.** Illustrated by Alfred Fredericks. 5s.

MAC KENNA, S. J.—**Plucky Fellows.** A Book for Boys. With 6 Illustrations. Fifth Edition. Crown 8vo, 3s. 6d.

REANEY, Mrs. G. S.—**Waking and Working ;** or, From Girlhood to Womanhood. New and Cheaper Edition. With a Frontispiece. Crown 8vo, 3s. 6d.

Blessing and Blessed : a Sketch of Girl Life. New and Cheaper Edition. Crown 8vo, 3s. 6d.

Rose Gurney's Discovery. A Book for Girls. Dedicated to their Mothers. Crown 8vo, 3s. 6d.

English Girls : Their Place and Power. With Preface by the Rev. R. W. Dale. Fourth Edition. Fcap. 8vo, 2s. 6d.

Just Anyone, and other Stories. Three Illustrations. Royal 16mo, 1s. 6d.

Sunbeam Willie, and other Stories. Three Illustrations. Royal 16mo, 1s. 6d.

Sunshine Jenny, and other Stories. Three Illustrations. Royal 16mo, 1s. 6d.

STOCKTON, Frank R.—A Jolly Fellowship. With 20 Illustra‑
tions. Crown 8vo, 5*s*.

STORR, Francis, and TURNER, Hawes.—Canterbury Chimes;
or, Chaucer Tales re‑told to Children. With 6 Illustrations from
the Ellesmere Manuscript. Third Edition. Fcap. 8vo, 3*s*. 6*d*.

STRETTON, Hesba.—David Lloyd's Last Will. With 4 Illustra‑
tions. New Edition. Royal 16mo, 2*s*. 6*d*.

Tales from Ariosto Re‑told for Children. By a Lady. With 3
Illustrations. Crown 8vo, 4*s*. 6*d*.

WHITAKER, Florence.—Christy's Inheritance. A London Story.
Illustrated. Royal 16mo, 1*s*. 6*d*.